# The Million Dollar Decision

---

## Get Out of the Rigged Game of Investing and Add a Million to Your Net Worth

---

## *Robert Rolih*

EMBASSY BOOKS
www.embassybooks.in

**The Million Dollar Decision © Robert Rolih**

First Edition 2019

Published in India by:
Embassy Book Distributors
120, Great Western Building,
Maharashtra Chamber of Commerce Lane,
Fort, Mumbai 400 023, India
Tel: (+9122) -30967415, 22819546
Email: info@embassybooks.in
www.embassybooks.in


Distribution Centres
Mumbai, Ahmedabad, Bangalore, Kolkata, Chennai,
Hyderabad, New Delhi, Pune

ISBN: 978-93-88247-67-2


Printed & Bound in India by Repro India Ltd., Navi Mumbai

# More Praise for Robert Rolih and *The Million Dollar Decision*

"The Million Dollar Decision is a really unusual book about investing. It's unusual because it's seriously easy to read, eye-opening and immediately actionable. If you don't know the first thing about investing (and even if you're a seasoned investor) you'll find this guide to be frightening, thought-provoking and incredibly useful, with its play-by-play instructions on making your own Million Dollar Decision. Highly recommended and required reading for my friends and clients."

–Matthew Kimberley, author of *How To Get A Grip*

"Wow! You probably knew that the financial industry is not your friend. But you probably never imagined just how much money you are losing when investing because of it. In this landmark book, Robert Rolih gives you a surprisingly simple solution that will help you win the money game of life. If you are investing, or if you are thinking about investing, read this book now. It will change your life and save you a lot of money."

–Brian Tracy, international bestselling author of *Maximum Achievement*

"This is one of the rare, if not the only, investing book that reads like a page-turner novel. If you care about your financial future, and you don't want to get ripped off by the financial industry, read it now. Every day you postpone reading it, you are losing money without even being aware of it."

–Daven Michaels, New York Times bestselling author of *Outsource Smart*

"Stop giving away your hard-earned money to the financial industry! The Million Dollar Decision is a must read for busy professionals that want to get the best possible investing returns with minimum effort. You're going to love it, it's simply amazing!"

–Jesse Eker, Managing Director, Harv Eker International

"This book is amazing. I thought I knew almost all there is to know about investing. But I put my emotions aside and learned from Robert's expertise. That's when I realized that if an investment or financial product is being marketed heavily, who benefits the most? Probably not me! When Robert showed me the true cost of fees and the opportunity cost of my time over a long period, I was stunned! I took immediate action to bring my investments in line with Robert's recommendations. Now I'm aggressively building my business and passively investing for the long run. I believe this book really will be a Million Dollar Decision for me!"

–Ralph Brogden, bestselling author, marketing and media strategist

"I think the right education is very important because most people DO think they know everything and then when they hit the world of investing they clam up and freak out. They end up making bad decisions or no decisions at all. Robert's book truly educates the reader and keeps their attention throughout the entire book. I highly suggest everyone read this book – it's phenomenal."

–Anthony Morrison, author and self-made millionaire

"Amazing. Surprising. Original. Fun. Definitely, a landmark book that will shatter every assumption you have about investing and managing your money."

–Kevin Green, wealth coach, one of the UK's largest
residential property landlords, kevingreen.co.uk

"This book WILL change the way you invest! I just wish I had this book sooner in my life, but better late than never. I must say that I never thought an investment book could be such an easy, fun read. This is a must read!"

–Anik Singal, founder and CEO of Lurn, Inc. & film producer

"Robert's stark look at how to build your wealth is critical for serious wealth growers to understand. Your money is your responsibility, and this book will change the way you think about building wealth – forever!"

–Kane Minkus, founder of Industry Rockstar, bestselling author, recipient of the International Brand Laurette Award

"Today, there are thousands of investing books on the market. Some of them are good, some are bad. Some of them are written for experts, while some of them are for a general audience. But none of them will give you a simpler and more effective solution on how to invest. Imagine if you didn't know how to drive a car yesterday, and today you're able to compete with the pros in the Daytona 500. That's the result that this book allows you to achieve!"

–Robert G. Allen, #1 New York Times bestselling author of *The One Minute Millionaire*

"The minute I picked up this book, I was impressed. If you want to build wealth and invest your money wisely, this book will show you the right moves."

–Fred Lam, author of The Better Business Mogul Blog

"Stunning and fun. Robert Rolih gives you a new, counter-intuitive philosophy for financial and investing success. This book is a true lifesaver."

–Raymond Aaron, New York Times bestselling author

"I love this book .... it is engaging, funny and yet, deadly serious as Robert busts the myths and dispels the growing "get rich quick" culture that is pervading the investment world. The section on the six dark forces of investing is glaringly obvious - but only after you read Robert's explanation and then smack your palm to your forehead. Robert not only dispels the myths, he also explains how you can generate long lasting wealth, providing for your future, your retirement and a legacy for your family. This book is a must read."

–Vicki Wusche, author, speaker, one of the Telegraph's 25 Most Influential People in Property VickiWusche.com

"If you only read one investing book in your lifetime, this is the one. When my coaching clients ask me about investing, I just tell them to read Robert's book, and they won't go wrong."

–Sai Blackbyrn, author and coach

"This book is a great guide to the crazy jungle of investing. I realized that nobody could take care of my money as well as me. That is why I'm happy I had the opportunity to learn from this book and make the Million Dollar Decision. Read it! It can change your financial life forever!"

–Lorand Soares Szasz, bestselling author, business growth expert

"Being a doctor of medicine, I have never enjoyed books about personal finance, investing or business. Interestingly enough, my family situation changed, and I needed some investing advice. By a stroke of magic, I got your book a few weeks ago, and I started to read it.

Usually, when I do something serious, I turn off the phone to get rid of interruptions, emails and social media. When I started to read your book, I had my Wi-Fi on, because I still was thinking that this would be a boring book. But very soon I was so drawn in, I was not paying any attention to anything else. Even my strict sleeping schedule got screwed up because of my interest in your book. This was the first book about personal finance and investing that I not only read from cover to cover, but I also used to change my investing plans. Now I realize the reasons why I lost money in the past. I cannot thank you enough for the information in your book."

–Dylaan Dowlati, MD, MBA-HCM, medical solution specialist

# Table of Contents

# Why You NEED to Read This Book Today...

If you are reading this book, it's probably because you know that investing should be a part of your money management goals.

Perhaps you want to accumulate enough money to have financial peace of mind when you retire. Maybe you want to finance your children's education, increase the financial security of your family or create a passive income stream.

There is just one problem.

You don't know how to do it. You don't know which products to choose. You don't know when to invest. Maybe you are even scared to invest because it seems so complicated and you don't understand all the confusing investing mumbo jumbo out there.

Of course, there is an army of experts out there ready to help you. Perhaps you will hire a financial adviser or wealth manager? Maybe you will trust your banker's or broker's advice.

Sounds logical, a no-brainer. What else could you do?

But that would be the **biggest financial mistake** you can make and will probably **cost you over one million dollars** in the long run.

I made the same mistake too.

And the main reason why I wrote this book is to help you avoid it. Too much is at stake when you make the decision on how to invest. Your wealth, future, and peace of mind are on the line.

In this book, I will explain how the financial industry rigged the game of investing, so you **automatically lose the majority of your future returns** – without even being aware of it.

I will show you how most financial advisers, gurus and other "experts" are working hard to help you make the wrong investing decisions – so they can profit from it. By the time you digest this book, the realization will hit that you and your family can easily lose more than a million dollars if you trust the advice of most investing "experts."

I have a feeling that you will be shocked. Maybe even angry and hurt because you will see that the people that you thought are helping you, are in reality destroying your financial future. But that's OK. Because, like Bob Dylan said, "Behind every beautiful thing, there's some kind of pain."

And last but not least, I will share with you these details and secret subtleties that will enable you to **fire your financial adviser,** take **control** of your money and investments and **outperform the pros -** while spending only a few **hours per year.**

Sound impossible?

Don't worry. The rest of this book will show you how and why it can be **so easy:**

In chapter 1, "Rewind << The Rocking Chair, The Giant and the Deadliest Investing Mistake You Can Make," I will show you how I lost a lot of money because I trusted financial advisers and wealth managers and how you can avoid the same fate.

In chapter 2, "Six Dark Forces of Investing: You Are Losing Money Without Even Knowing It," you will get to know the deadly forces of investing and how to avoid them. If you don't learn what these forces are, you will never be able to invest profitably, and you will lose money without even being aware of it.

Chapter 3, "Financial Success Formula: How Most People Get It All Wrong?" reveals the most important formula of your financial life. This is an entirely new philosophy on personal finance and investing that will, quite literally, save you financially. If you have adult children, you will want to share the key points of this chapter with them right away.

In chapter 4, "Just Don't Sign Here: The Perils of Financial Safety?" I will share with you the keys to financial safety and reveal to you how some of the most popular insurance products can be quite harmful to your financial future.

Chapter 5, "Gone with the Wind: Where Do Your Long-Term Investing Returns End Up?" takes you behind the scenes of the financial industry. You will learn the most powerful investing concept and its dark side, that is being used by the financial industry to obliterate your investing returns. Plus, I will share with you a simple solution that will enable you to get out of the rigged game of investing.

In chapter 6, "Short-Term Investing Slaughterhouse: Gurus on Hard Drugs Helping You to Part with Your Money," I will reveal perhaps the most lethal investing money drain. Just this knowledge alone can save you thousands of dollars and years of time.

Chapter 7, "Fast Forward >> The Simple Way to Win the Financial Game of Life," is all about getting your financial act together. Here, I will show you how quickly you can save one million dollars - just by following the principles in this book.

And the bonus Chapter, "My Three Best Financial Breakthrough Cheat Codes," will give you some of my best secret weapons that can help you to increase your income so you have more money to invest.

By reading this book you will:

**1. Never need to seek the advice of a financial advisor or banker.** In fact, just by reading this book, you will know more about personal finance and investing than 95% of so-called experts and advisers.

**2. Have total confidence in yourself when investing.** I believe that if you want to invest successfully, you first need to understand the financial products, or assets, that are available. That is why I will explain everything in a very easy to understand language with a lot of examples. Even if you don't have a clue about personal finance and investing, this book will make sense to you.

**3. Save more than one million dollars.** Managing and investing your money in a way that the financial industry teaches you, will eventually lead to your financial collapse. Learning from someone who has been there will save you and your family more than one million dollars in the upcoming years.

**4. Outperform even the experts in just a couple of hours per year.** When you apply my system of investing, you will see that great investing returns are not the result of the quantity of time you put in. Quite the contrary; with the knowledge you will receive here, you will be able to outperform the vast majority of investors in just a couple of hours per year!

**5. Save a ton of time.** Time is money. If you spend lots of time investing, you have less time for your family, business, hobbies and fun. So, what kind of life would you rather have: a life where you spend hours and hours each day watching the charts on your computer screen and reading boring corporate reports? Or a life where money is working for you passively, and you get time for travel, hobbies, your family or to focus on other money-making activities?

## A Quick Warning

But let me warn you: this book is **not** for people who are struggling financially. It's **not** a book on how to make more money – although the philosophy I teach will indirectly allow you to increase your income. It's **not** a book on how to save three dollars per day by not buying the things you love. It's also **not** a book on how to get out of debt or how to budget. And most of all, it's not a book on how to use coupons to save some pennies while grocery shopping.

This is a book for people who **already make a decent amount of money** and want to significantly **increase their net worth** by starting to invest or by changing the way they invest. This book is for people who already know that investing is a must and want to get the **best possible ROI (Return on Investment)**. It's for people who highly **value their time**, and want to be 100% sure that their financial security is taken care of and that their invested money is working hard for them and not for the financial industry.

So, if you see yourself in that description, there is a life-changing journey in front of us.

Prepare for takeoff!

Robert Rolih

# Foreword
# by Robert G. Allen

**I** first met Robert Rolih in 2014 when we shared a stage at a business conference. Usually, while waiting for my speaking slot, I'm focused on my presentation and have little interest in the speaker on stage. But this time was different.

Even though I've written some of the largest selling personal finance books in history, Robert's message struck me hard. His advice on how to invest and set up the money that comes in and out of your life was just fantastic—a total financial paradigm shift.

On top of that, his advice was also simple, interesting, fun and imaginative, which is quite the opposite of how investing experts usually present their ideas.

When Robert told me that he intended to write a book about his topic, I was delighted. I think that the world really needs to hear his message. You need to hear his message. If you don't, you will lose a ton of money and possibly even jeopardize your financial security.

In my book *Multiple Streams of Income,* I teach readers how to craft a wealth-building plan and how to make small monthly investments that can grow into a million-dollar nest egg. In *The Million Dollar Decision,* Robert Rolih upgrades this concept and shows you that most investing strategies will, in reality, wipe out your investing account, especially if you trust financial advisers to make investing decisions for you.

At first, the title of the book's claim will seem inflated or unrealistic, but as you dive deeper into the book, you'll realize that even an average family loses more than one million dollars in their lifetime thanks to the financial industry. And that is scary.

Today, there are thousands of investing books on the market. Some of them are good, some are bad. Some of them are written for experts, while some of them are for a general audience. But none of them will give you a simpler and more effective solution on how to invest.

If you're a **complete investing novice,** this book will show you how easy investing can be, and how you can outperform the vast majority of professional investors in no time. It will guide you around all the pitfalls and roadblocks on your way to financial success. It will be the shortcut that will help you get the best possible investing returns without going through years and years of learning. Imagine if you didn't know how to drive a car yesterday, and today you're able to compete with the pros in the Daytona 500. That's the result that this book allows you to achieve!

If you are **already investing with the help of financial advisers or brokers,** you will finally discover the true cost of their services. And believe me, you are in for a surprise. When you finish reading this book, you will probably wish you had known the information contained within ten years ago.

And if you are **actively trading the markets,** this book could be a wake-up call for you. Too many people spend years of their lives chasing above average returns only to find out that the Promised Land is not there, and they end up losing their health, wealth and relationships in the process.

Investing is a must for all of us. But without the right knowledge, you're not investing; you're gambling with little or no chance of success. This book will give you everything you need to make the best possible investing choices and avoid becoming another victim of the financial industry.

Like the title promises, reading this book could easily be worth a million or more for you and your family. That is why I urge you to read this book like your life depended on it! Reading it will be one of the best decisions you ever made.

Read it now!

Robert G. Allen, #1 New York Times bestselling author
Creating Wealth
Nothing Down
Multiple Streams of Income
The One Minute Millionaire

*"Success does not consist in never making mistakes but in never making the same one a second time."*

– George Bernard Shaw

# Chapter 1

Rewind << The Rocking Chair, The Giant and the Deadliest Investing Mistake You Can Make

**T**here are many mistakes you can make in your life. Most of them are pretty harmless. Some of them are worth making, just for the sake of gaining valuable experience. Some of them are costly but have just a short-term impact on one isolated area of your life.

And then some mistakes can have an **overwhelming effect** on your life. These errors can wreak havoc on your life, and the decision on **how to invest** your money is one of them. It has far reaching consequences that affect your wealth, health, family, emotional well-being and your overall quality of life.

I learned the most important lesson about investing and managing my money the hard way – by making that kind of mistake. In the grand scheme of things, it would not matter much if only a few people in the world made this mistake. But sadly, **the lion's share of investors make this error.** And the worst part is that they are not even aware of it.

In this chapter, I want to share with you how I made this mistake. Knowledge is power, and by learning from my mistakes, you will save an enormous amount of money and a lot of headaches.

Believe me…it's not worth making this kind of mistake just for the sake of experience.

## *A Boy with a Pair of Old Jeans and an Impossible Dream*

I earned my first six-figure after-tax income in my late 20s. That was a lot of money, considering I lived in Slovenia, an ex-socialist country with the population of only 2 million, where the average income was less than $12,000 at the time. Needless to say, life was good.

But then things changed. In the next few years, I lost most of my money.

When people lose a lot of money, the reasons are usually extravagant spending, gambling, medical problems or bad business decisions. My reason was surprisingly different.

At that time, life suddenly started to get ugly. And as I reflected on my situation I felt like the wheels of time turned and brought me back to where my adult life started...

It was spring of 1994. If you were with me then, you would see me sitting on an old wooden rocking chair in front of a modest house.

We are in a backwater village, with a population of 215. The sun is about to set. The air is warm, the birds are chirping, and there is a sweet scent of flowers in the air — the perfect day! If you look around, you see a lot of trees and grey houses scattered everywhere. The house behind us stands out, though. It has bright orange bricks and it doesn't have a façade yet.

I wore a washed-out t-shirt that was once blue, and my only pair of jeans. These kinds of clothes were not in fashion yet...so I was not popular with the girls — as you can imagine.

At that time in my life, I wanted all sorts of things (like most teenagers do), and I can still remember my father, a tough guy with a Jimi Hendrix haircut, repeatedly saying, with a raised voice, "No, Robert! We cannot afford it! We don't have enough money."

As you look at me, you notice that I am reading a book. You step closer and focus on the book cover. There is the author's photo on the cover, and you instantly recognize him – a leading business authority.

You see a shy smile on my face as I am rocking in my chair, with my eyes closed. All of a sudden I drift off into a daydream…

I'm having a delicious dinner with the author of the book in an expensive restaurant. He is tall, confident, with some wrinkles and grey hair. We eat and talk about business for an hour. As we are about to leave, he looks me straight in the eyes, and says, "Robert, you are such a great, young guy. Here is a check for one million dollars. Go ahead and start your own business, like you have always wanted; buy a nice house for your parents and have some fun."

At that moment, as I open my eyes, reality hits me, and I start to rant, "Robert, wake up! Stop dreaming! You are just a poor boy from a backwater village, in a country that most people don't even know exists, and you will never, ever meet a famous person like this. Let alone have dinner with him as friends!"

Now, have you ever dreamed of a better life, of achieving some big goals, and then said something similar to yourself?

I bet you have.

But life sometimes works in mysterious ways, doesn't it?

## *The Stage is Set*

Fast forward to 2005. You are sitting in the seventh row of a big, amphitheater-style conference room. The room is impressive, both in size and in attendance. It is packed full. You see famous CEOs, entrepreneurs and managers talking and shaking hands. There is an aura of expectation in the air.

Then, there is breathless silence.

As you look at the stage, you see me, the conference organizer, coming up on the stage. And in the wings, there is this tall, confident-looking man with some wrinkles and grey hair.

As I hit the center of the stage, I go: "Ladies and gentlemen! Please welcome to the stage, the legendary public speaker and bestselling author... Brian Tracy!"

As Brian started his talk, I sat down in the first row and prepared to make a lot of notes. However, I could not focus. My head was overflowing with thoughts and emotions. That moment was like winning the Olympic gold medal for the very first time.

As a teenager, when I read Brian's books, I had dreams of achieving something meaningful in my life. I also dreamt of getting rich and being able to afford all the things I wanted. But I never seriously believed that I had what it took to make it happen. I had no particular talents, my IQ was average and my family was poor. So, you can probably imagine how I felt when my business that I started from scratch in a student dorm room, culminated in organizing a big event with Brian Tracy. Just the revenue from that event was more than an average person in my country made in his or her entire career. I didn't know if Brian would be happy about my focus level during the first minutes of his seminar, but I couldn't help it. I was just too excited!

So, could life get any better?

It could.

But, it could also get worse.

## *The Big Problem with Financial Success*

It was nice to be successful and have a lot of money. But then a challenge presented itself.

I was not the kind of guy who would go on a spending spree as soon as I got some money. I knew that investing a part of the money I made was a must; I knew that I needed to secure my financial future in case anything bad happened and start putting money away for my retirement.

Nevertheless, there was a problem: I was an entrepreneur, and I did not know anything about investing. Furthermore, I hated investing and personal finance. I did not want to get my hands "dirty" by immersing myself in Excel spreadsheets, floods of numbers and financial news. I also didn't have the time to learn about the different financial products…

So I trusted…

Yes, you guessed it right.

I trusted in financial advisers.

Month after month, year after year, I gave them my money. They promised to take good care of it, and multiply it with all sorts of long-term and short-term investing products.

I said to myself, "Great! That's taken care of for good! Let's go back to business! My money is in good hands now."

A few years later, my wife and I had a little chat about our money.

"We are doing great in business, but still, it would be nice to see how much money we have," she remarked.

"Ok, seems like a good idea. It is always good to know the facts," I agreed.

I then asked my financial advisers, who had been giving me investing guidance for the last few years, to send me account statements.

The white envelopes with the names of the investing companies arrived by post. I was excited about the prospect of opening them and seeing the money that has accumulated because of my wise decision to hire the best advisers.

I opened the first envelope... "Hmmm, this must be a mistake!"

Second one: "Is there a zero missing?"

Third one: "Aaagghhh! Are you serious?!?"

Unfortunately, for me, there were no mistakes: my money was almost gone. At the time, I couldn't even comprehend why and how that had happened. I thought to myself, "Is this really happening? I'm working hard day and night in my business, I earn a lot of money and now most of it is gone?"

I was devastated. Just imagine how you would feel if you had lost most of your money. In fact, I lost more than 80% of all the money I invested.

For a few weeks, I could hardly force myself to go to work. It was one of those moments in life when you do not know with whom to be angry — the people who did it, or yourself because you let it happen.

But in hindsight, maybe I was lucky that this happened to me and that I got my financial reality check at that time. Many people find out that they have much less money than they expected in their retirement accounts when it's already too late.

## *The Insight That Changed It All*

Have you ever had an experience where you needed something in life, and it just appeared out of thin air?

Magic? Luck? Forces of nature? Energy? God?

Or just a coincidence?

I don't know. But it happened to me at that time.

I was very lucky that Brian Tracy was a speaker at one of my seminars again. I invited him to dinner after the event — and this time, it was not just a daydream.

Brian is a very fascinating person. He is always commanding the conversation and giving advice. That is why my conversation with him seemed a little odd. We spoke for 20 minutes ... well, I talked, and he just nodded from time to time.

After I had shared all my financial frustrations with him, he looked me directly in the eyes and said something that changed my life forever. It could change your life, too.

"Robert, it doesn't matter how much you earn. All that matters is whether you have the skills to manage your money and to invest it."

That was a pivotal moment in my life. At that time, I realized, "I don't have these skills. I blindly trusted the financial industry and advisers."

# "Blindly trusting financial experts is like trusting your chickens to Mr. Fox."

@RobertRolih #MillionDollarDecision

That led me to make perhaps the most important decision in my life. I made a promise that, no matter how much time and money it takes, I would become one of the most financially literate people in the world.

That is why, in the following seven years, I invested heavily in my financial education. I took tons of investment courses; I read more than 300 books. I invested years of my life and more than $100,000, just for seminar fees. I was on a mission, and I thought that I had it all figured out.

With all that education, you would think that I could never make investing mistakes again. But that was not the case. Do you know they say that the devil is in the details?

Later, I found out those details that nobody talked about in all those books and in all those courses. And I realized that if you didn't know these crucial details, nothing else mattered, because the financial industry would crush you.

Only after extensive research and working with some industry insiders was I able to pinpoint what these details were – and why it was important to know them.

When you know these details, and you act accordingly, then investing becomes straightforward and effortless. And best of all, you realize that you don't need more than a couple of hours per year to beat the pros at their own game.

Are you ready to learn what these carefully guarded secrets are?

Then join me in the next chapter, where we will take a look at the main six reasons why people lose money when investing.

## *The Million Dollar Action Plan*

Having mentors is one of the common characteristics shared by the most successful people in the world. A great mentor helps you reach your goals faster than you ever could by yourself. Throughout my career, I've been fortunate to have a lot of great mentors, and Brian Tracy is the one who had the greatest impact on my life.

As my gift to you, I prepared a summary of the seven best strategies for increasing income I learned from him.

With your purchase of The Million Dollar Decision, you also receive complimentary access to the members-only website with bonus materials and important additional resources. To get access, visit www.MillionDollarDecisionBook.com/bonus now. I believe that this bonus could prove to be priceless to you – as long as you apply the strategies within.

*"If I had an hour to solve a problem I'd spend 55 minutes thinking about the problem and 5 minutes thinking about solutions."*

– Albert Einstein

# Chapter 2

## Six Dark Forces of Investing: You Are Losing Money Without Even Knowing It

The biggest problem of investing is that we are not aware of the problem that is sitting right underneath our noses.

When my business took off, I frequently hired advisors and consultants who helped me to grow my company and make it successful. That strategy worked wonders for me. When I started to invest, I thought that the same would apply to investing. I trusted financial advisers, bankers and investing gurus. I thought that the world of investing was fair and that I could win the financial game of life by trusting their advice.

I lost a lot of money because of that, and I am not alone. From my experience of talking to thousands of people who attended my seminars, I can say that most investors are in the same position as I was. Most investors think that their invested money works for them; but in reality, it works mostly for the financial industry. And when they realize it, it's usually too late.

So, before you invest another cent, you need to be aware of the hidden problems that we all face when investing, if you are not, your chances of getting good returns are close to zero.

I spent years studying the workings of the financial industry, and I found six major problems that people face when investing their money. These problems are the reasons why most investors lose a very big part of their potential returns. I call them *The Six Dark Forces of Investing*.

Get to know them, and Darth Vader will seem like a good guy to you.

## Dark Force #1: The Commission Camouflage Effect

To understand the first dark force that 'helps' investors lose a large part of their potential investing returns, we need to go to Las Vegas.

I don't gamble, but I like to visit Las Vegas from time to time. It's a nice experience, and it can be fun.

I'm writing this chapter from my hotel room overlooking the Vegas Strip. I will be staying here for five days, attending a mastermind event with fellow public speakers and business owners.

You probably agree with me that when in Vegas, you can hardly avoid casinos. It's just amazing to see all these people putting money in the slot machines and playing Roulette. People are always drawn to the opportunities that offer big rewards for little or no work, although they know that most players lose money. Maybe a few people get lucky sometimes, but in the end, it's the house that always wins.

The house has an edge, and there is a mathematical certainty that it will earn 2 to 25 percent of all the money that goes through that casino. But this is actually OK — when we are in a casino, we know our odds. We are aware that our chances of winning, over the long run, are next to none.

Now you are probably wondering, "what do casinos have to do with investing and retirement planning?" The answer is a lot. We all know that we have to invest if we want to provide for ourselves in old age, for our family, to have a better lifestyle and make our money work for us.

We're also trying to win the game – that means getting good returns on our investments, such as stocks, funds, bonds and other financial instruments.

We also know that the investing world has a 'house' with an edge — 'the house' always gets some commissions and fees. And again, that's OK, as long as we are aware of that.

But now comes the ugly part. Investors are mostly unaware that the house not only has an edge, but that it has also rigged the game. And by 'the house,' I mean the financial institutions, fund managers, financial advisors, brokers, etc.

## "If you are playing the rigged game of investing, the house always wins."

@RobertRolih #MillionDollarDecision

They have rigged the game in such a cunning way that even experienced investors don't notice it most of the time. Because of that, most investors lose 50 to 70 percent of all the investing gains they would get over the course of their investing career.

What does this mean for you as an investor? Simply put, if your investments could bring you a gain of, let's say $100, over the long run, you are getting only $30 to $50, because the game is rigged. Ouch! Think about that for a second. You are now 60 years old, and instead of seeing a million dollar gain in your investment account, you only have $300,000 or $500,000. Think of all you could do with the difference: buy a beach house, retire early, do what you enjoy most… the possibilities are endless.

But you can't, because the house got your money!

Now you are probably wondering how does this happen? How did they rig the investing game?

First is the way that the commission and fee system works. We all know that there are some fees and commissions associated with any investment product. But what we can hardly grasp is how the commissions influence our long-term investing returns.

Let me give you an example. If you invest your money in a simple mutual fund, you are paying a 2% annual fee, give or take. And this doesn't sound like much. When your financial advisor tells you that you are paying a 2% annual fee, your brain says "OK… this is not a problem. They take 2 and I keep 98."

Right?

Wrong!

The problem is that our brain can only do simple calculations: "2% out of $1,000? Hmmm… 1% of $1,000 equals $10, so 2% must be $20. No problem! We did that in school! I'm a math genius!"

But, when you add a longer time period – and most investors are investing for the long run – maybe 10, 20, 30 or even 40 years, our brain just can't process the math anymore. If I ask you how much is 2% deducted annually for 30 years in a market that grows by 8% on average, your brain goes, "Are you kidding me? I'm not R2-D2!"

Our brains are just not wired to calculate complex calculations like this. And that is perfectly normal. Most people wouldn't be able to calculate this, even with the help of a computer.

That is why we subconsciously make some approximations and assumptions: "If 2% of my invested money in one year is a small number, then a 2% annual fee can't be a serious problem over the long run."

But unfortunately, our brains fail us badly in this case. The financial industry knows this and takes full advantage of it. That is why they will never explain the effect of commissions over the long run to you. Even if you have the best financial adviser, it just doesn't happen.

A small annual commission is a devil in disguise. In the best case, it can cause you a lot of financial problems when you retire, and in the worst case, it can wipe you out. We will go into all the details, and I will give you some specific numbers later in chapter 5, but for now, just remember, that, as a rule of thumb, a 2% annual fee halves your retirement pot in the long run.

Now let me ask you a question: What would you say if your financial adviser offered you a financial product where you got to keep only half of the future returns?

If you are like me, you would run away as fast as you could.

But most investors don't, and buy their financial adviser a box of chocolates because he or she provided them with great advice. Why? Because nobody told them about what I call the "Commission Camouflage Effect."

The Commission Camouflage Effect states that small annual commissions tend to eat a large part of our investing returns over the long run. It's one of the deadliest concepts in investing, and just by getting to know it, you can save a surprisingly large amount of money. For most investors, this amount can easily go into the six-figure range.

**Exhibit 2.1** The Commission Camouflage Effect of a 2% annual fee over the long run

FALSE ASSUMPTION OUR BRAIN MAKES
"I KEEP 98 OUT OF 100"

REALITY
"I KEEP 50 OUT OF 100"

Let me summarize. The first Dark Force of Investing is the destructive power of the Commission Camouflage Effect that makes you believe that you are paying a small fee when you are, in fact, paying a very large one. Because of that effect, I sometimes joke that the odds of winning in Las Vegas are greater than on Wall Street. Unfortunately, there is a lot of truth in that claim.

## *Dark Force #2: Reward Corruption*

Once upon a time, there was an insurance intermediary company that employed a couple of hundred insurance brokers. Life was good. The agents were meeting their clients, identifying their needs and advising them on which insurance policies to use for their situations. They were happy; the customers were happy.

But then something happened. The insurance company they represented created a new product. A whole life insurance policy where a part of your monthly payment goes toward insurance, and a part towards investment in mutual funds.

There was something fascinating about this product that made quite a stir with all the brokers. The sales commissions they would get when they sold this product were three times higher compared to any other product.

Human nature quickly took hold, and in a period of one month, all the brokers focused on selling this product. After all, who wouldn't grab a carrot like this!

All of a sudden, this product became a solution for almost all the needs of their customers. The typical sales approach was, "Customer, for any problem you might have, we will sell you this product. It's the best and the only option. Buy it now! Resistance is futile!" And it sold well because brokers were very motivated to sell it. A big payout was just around the corner for them.

The CEO of the company was ecstatic. He hadn't seen profits like this for a long time. And when something sells well – why not give it an additional kick.

So he organized a sales competition. The broker who sold the most policies in the next quarter would win a six month lease on a new Ferrari. If the brokers were very motivated before, they were on fire now.

Now, all this would not be so bad if the product was a good product for the customers. But the reality was that this product was one of the worst financial products out there, charging enormous commissions and fees.

The second Dark Force of Investing is the reward systems of most financial institutions. These reward systems can motivate their employees and partners to be biased and highly motivated to sell something that is not right for the customer and often leads to unethical or corrupt behavior.

When employees sell high commission products, they make more money, and customers make less. It's that simple. The higher the commissions and fees, the worse off are the customers. That is why the most popular financial products are the worst ones for the customer. I call this the Chain of Financial Ruin.

**Exhibit 2.2** The Chain of Financial Ruin

It is the main reason why the financial industry is one of the most profitable industries around. In the U.S., it employs less than 5% of the population, but it produces more than 30% of all the corporate profits, according to the U.S. Bureau of Economic Analysis[1]. How is that profit made? From the customers, of course.

## Dark Force #3: Bad Guys Setting the Rules of the Game

I met with someone not too long ago. He was a typical alpha male in his 50's. He was wearing an expensive dark grey suit with a black tie. If you talked to him, you could detect a hint of a superiority complex.

"We put Apple stock in every managed portfolio," he said. "We think that Apple stock will underperform in the future, but it's better to have it in all of our customer's portfolios."

"Why would you do that if you think that Apple's stock will underperform?" I replied, surprised.

"Do you know the saying that nobody ever got fired for choosing IBM?" he said without a sense of wrongdoing. "People love the Apple brand and their products, that is why it looks good to have Apple in their portfolios. It's good for the sales! But if the stock underperforms, the customers will not blame us for choosing it. So it's a win-win proposition for us. We sell more and they will not blame us if the stock doesn't do well."

I must say that at first I couldn't decide if he was joking or if he was serious. Unfortunately, for his clients, he was serious. I think that was when I gave up hope that the financial industry even remotely cared about the customer.

I wanted to say to him, "Wouldn't you rather take 30 minutes of your time to record a video educating your clients about why you don't put Apple in their portfolios?" but I saw that it would be useless.

It really doesn't matter what will happen with the Apple stock. Maybe it will go well in the future, maybe not. I don't know. But I'm sure as hell not in good hands when I hire a financial adviser or wealth manager that thinks like this – and neither are you!

The third Dark Force of Investing is that there are just too many bad guys in the industry. Lack of ethics is so ingrained in most companies that they are not even aware of it any more. It's just a normal way of doing business. In short: they don't really care about their customers – about you – all they care about are their sales targets and profits.

Case in point: the Wells Fargo shocking scandal, where federal regulators found out that Wells Fargo employees secretly created millions of unauthorized bank and credit card accounts from 2011

- 2016[2]. In order to meet their sales targets, employees would, for example, create a new savings account for a customer and then transfer funds from his or her existing checking account into the new bogus savings account without customer's permission. Wells Fargo bank admitted the "widespread illegal practices," fired more than 5,000 employees, and agreed to pay $185 million in fines.

Perhaps the most worrisome thing about all this is the sheer scope of this scandal. When more than 5,000 employees are involved in illegal behavior, you have to think that similar activities were probably a normal way of doing business at the bank. And, when you think about that, you have to wonder how many illegal and unethical activities that we don't know about are really going on in the financial sector.

# "Lack of ethics is so ingrained in the financial industry that they are not even aware of it any more. It's just business as usual for them."

### @RobertRolih #MillionDollarDecision

When I was young I watched a western movie, where the last scene of the movie stuck in my mind for a long time. In this scene, the protagonists of the movie, the good guys, ended up surrounded by an army of bad guys and were killed, one by one.

Even though the good guys fought bravely, there were just too many bad guys out there.

I can still remember how bad I felt at that time. I was still young and I believed that good always prevailed. I believed that life was fair and that wrongdoings always got punished. But unfortunately, life is not always fair and bad guys do get away without punishment a lot of the time.

In my opinion a very similar thing is happening in the financial industry – there are just too many bad guys in the industry.

From my experience of observing and researching the industry, I was able to construct a chart that classifies people working in the financial industry depending on their behavior. Mind that this chart is just my estimation.

**Exhibit 2.3** People working in the financial industry

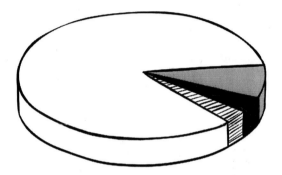

## The Bad Guys

First let's take a look at the dark gray part of the pie. These are the bad guys of the financial industry. They are not necessarily bad people. But in their business lives, they are not working for their clients' interests. They produce or sell financial products that are bringing in a lot of profit for them, but are very bad for clients. Or, they are giving harmful financial advice in order to profit for themselves.

So, these are the people who are producing and selling very bad financial products and they know it.

I once worked with a bank that hired me to train its sales staff. We talked about how important it is to believe that your product is the best solution for the client. During a break, one of the participants came to me and said, "Robert, I understand that you need to believe in your product, and, for most of our products, I believe that they are the best.

But a couple of weeks ago, we had a meeting with our sales manager, and he told us that we need to push a certain product. After that, he told us that this product has very high fees, and that he would never buy it for himself. Now, how can I recommend this product to my customers after that?"

Now…that is a good question!

## The Crooks

Next is the black part of our chart. These are the fraudsters who should be in jail. If the bad guys are operating legally, fraudsters or scheme artists are not. They are usually operating an illegal business practice called the Ponzi scheme.

**Exhibit 2.4** The Bad Guys and the Crooks

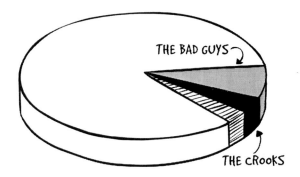

A Ponzi scheme is named after Charles Ponzi, who constructed one such scheme at the beginning of the 20th century. It's a pyramid scheme where the newest members of the group think that they invest money in a legitimate opportunity, but in reality, their money is not being invested – it's only used to pay people higher up in the pyramid.

One of the most famous Ponzi scheme operators was Bernard Madoff, who orchestrated the biggest Ponzi scheme to date and stole an estimated $20 to $65 billion from his investors[3].

Why do people invest in these kinds of schemes? Because they are drawn in with the promise of very high returns. In other words: greed. A Ponzi scheme operator is getting people to join by promising them 20%, 50% or even 100% return on their investments. And, on top of that, he is usually guaranteeing these returns.

## "When investing, greed can be your worst enemy."

### @RobertRolih #MillionDollarDecision

But the system needs a constant flow of new investors in order to exist, because the money is not really invested; it just flows to the top of the pyramid. And once the scam artist feels that enough money has been collected, he disappears – taking all the money with him. Ponzi schemes have ruined millions of financial lives. Don't let yours be next.

So how can you spot a Ponzi scheme? Your alarm should go off if somebody is offering you an investment that seems too good to be true. As a rule of thumb: if somebody promises or guarantees annual returns of 7% or more, it's probably a Ponzi scheme. Why? Because nobody can guarantee these kind of returns.

But are 10% or 50% per year returns possible? Yes, of course! Stocks have historically provided an annualized return of approximately 10%. But these returns are not constant. Some years can be great for stocks; and some years can be terrible.

Remember: you can get high returns of 50% or 100% in a short period of time when investing. But this always carries a lot of risk. So, if somebody tells you that you can get a 50% return on your investment, but you can also lose 30, 50 or 70% of your money - than it's OK. But if someone guarantees you returns like this, then something stinks!

## The Good Guys

The next slice of our pie is the smallest one. These are the good guys. Percentage wise, they are few, but they do exist!

These guys are producing financial products that are good for their clients. We'll talk about them later in the book.

## Clueless

And then we have the remaining – the largest – part of the pie. Approximately 85% of people working in the financial industry operate under the influence of the bad guys. This means that they are either employed by them, or rewarded by them. These are the salesmen, advisers, brokers and others who are selling financial products.

**Exhibit 2.5** People working in the financial industry (continued)

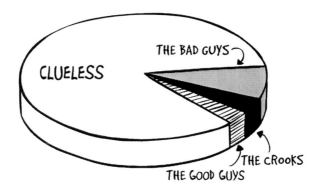

They are good people and they think that they are recommending viable investments to their clients but, unfortunately, they aren't. The problem is that they know only the nice parts of the story regarding the products they are promoting. Nobody has told them the bad parts. So, these guys are not bad guys. They are merely promoting what bad guys tell them to promote, and, in most cases, they do not even know that this is bad for the clients.

If I summarize: The third Dark Force of Investing is the sheer number of bad guys and people under their influence in the industry. Sometimes even those who think that they are really helping you can be a great hindrance to your financial well-being.

## *Dark Force #4: Fortune-Telling Investing Gurus*

There was a psychic with the strange name of Baba Vanga that predicted the 9/11 terrorist attacks. Even though the prediction she made was quite ambiguous, she received a lot of media attention.

A Zimbabwean preacher, Uebert Angel, correctly predicted the death of ex South African President Nelson Mandela. He got quite a bit of media attention.

Paul the Octopus (yes, this was really a common octopus and not a person) correctly predicted the results of eleven 2010 Soccer World Cup games. Are you were wondering how the octopus did that? Well, writing it on an aquarium wall would certainly be a feat! But that is not what happened. Paul's owners would present him with two boxes containing food. Each box was identical except for the fact that, on each box, there was a country flag of the competitors of an upcoming football match. Whichever box Paul ate from first would be considered his prediction for the winning team. Correct predictions brought him worldwide attention as an animal oracle.

John Poulson, now famous fund manager, correctly predicted the housing crash of 2007-2009. He made a lot of money and there was even a book, *The Greatest Trade Ever*, written about him.

Now here it starts to get interesting…

Baba Vanga is just one out of thousands of psychics who make predictions every year. 99% of them are wrong, but nobody writes about them. The headline that says, "Psychic X missed his last three predictions about the future," doesn't sell newspapers.

There are thousands of preachers and prophets who predict different events every year. The most popular ones are, of course, the ones about the end of the world. Now, as you are still alive reading this book, I assume that none of these predictions were correct.

After Paul the Octopus, there were thousands of other animals, including elephants, cats and even worms whose owners tried to predict the outcome of different sports tournaments and games. I guess you can figure how that turned out.

There are thousands of investing gurus writing articles, books and making predictions on TV about what will happen next with the stock market or the price of oil. How come the media forgets about them when they are proved wrong?

Even John Poulson's performance after his winning trades of 2007 is far below average. Let me just give you a short excerpt from a Bloomberg Business article about him from 2015[4]:

*"Billionaire John Paulson posted the second-worst trading year of his career in 2014 as a wrong-way energy bet added to declines tied to a failed merger and investments in Fannie Mae and Freddie Mac.*

*The worst performance was in the Advantage Plus fund, which plummeted 36 percent last year, two people with knowledge of the returns said...*

*The manager, who shot to fame after making $15 billion on the housing crisis in 2007, has struggled to regain its footing since 2011 when bets on the U.S. recovery went awry, losing money in all of its main strategies - including a 51 percent tumble in the Advantage Plus fund. Paulson also lost money in investments tied to gold and Europe's economy, causing assets to dwindle to $19 billion, half the peak in 2011."*

See the pattern here?

There are thousands of fund managers and gurus out there. Some of them get lucky in a certain period of time. They become famous. They start attracting a lot of new investors with fresh money. Then they run out of luck and start producing below average or even negative returns. So, all the people who started to invest with them, or who invested based on their recommendations, get burned. This has happened thousands of times in recent history and will happen again and again.

# "You only get to know which predictions will be correct afterwards. When it's too late."

### @RobertRolih #MillionDollarDecision

Let me illustrate this point with a simple thought experiment. Let's say that you have a thousand computers. They are all programmed to make one exact prediction about the next price-move of a randomly selected stock. For example, the stock is now at $7 and the first computer predicts that in one year it will be at $9, the second one forecasts it will be at $6.5 and so on.

Do you think that some predictions will come true? Sure they will! There is a mathematical probability that a small number of computers will hit the mark.

But will you jump around with your hands in the air claiming that the computers that hit the mark have predicting powers? And would you bet your retirement fund that their next prediction will be on target? Probably not.

So, whether you are Paul the Octopus, or John Paulson, you can just admit it: you were just lucky once or twice. I couldn't emphasize this more: the fact that somebody correctly predicted the last crisis, or the last big gold price-move, doesn't mean that he/she has reliable predicting abilities. He or she was just lucky.

Are there some exceptions? No. We have yet to find an investing guru who correctly predicted more than one or two big price movements or important events.

CXO Advisory Group has been collecting data from 68 market forecasters from 1998 to 2012. In that period of time, they collected more than 6,500 predictions made by these famous investing gurus and experts. Some of them predicted that a certain stock would go up or down and some predicted the course that the market, as a whole, would take. Then in a very comprehensive study, they analyzed if the predictions these forecasters made were right or wrong[5].

Now, if you were making 6,500 up or down predictions, you would probably end up being correct half of the time. This is the standard mathematical probability. 50% of your predictions would be proven right and 50% wrong.

But guess how the gurus fared…

There were some of the well-known names analyzed in that study. For example, Ben Zacks, the co-founder of the well-known Zacks Investment Research, and portfolio manager at Zacks Wealth Management Group, had a score of exactly 50%.

James Dines, founder of The Dines Letter newsletter, a guy who is often referred as "one of the most accurate and highly regarded security investment analysts today", was also correct only half of the time. That's really very accurate.

*I'M HAVING BETTER RESULTS THAN MOST HIGHLY PAID WALL STREET EXPERTS, AND ALL I GET IN RETURN ARE SOME LOUSY BANANAS!*

And, my favorite - Robert Prechter, known for his financial forecasts using the Elliott Wave Principle and author of multiple investing books. His score was… wait for it… 20.8%. Now, you really need a lot of bad luck for that.

And the average score across all of their predictions?

Most forecasters were right in the 40% to 60% range, with some deviations to the upper and lower side. So, the best score out of all forecasters was 68.8% and the lowest was 20.8%. That's exactly what you would expect from a random distribution – a typical bell curve.

And the average across all predictions was 46.9%. In less than half of their predictions, they were right. If you would employ monkeys to throw darts (unfortunately octopus doesn't throw darts), they would, on average, fare better than that.

**Exhibit 2.6** Guru accuracy

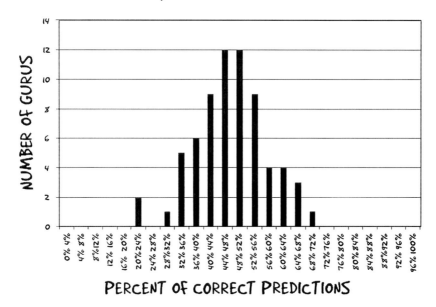

In other words – you can beat these famous investing gurus by just tossing a coin. Assuming that the coin toss is fair, heads and tails are equally likely. And 50% always beats 48%. It's that simple. So, next time you see a famous guru making predictions, simply ignore him or her. He/she just wants to get some media attention and sell some more books or events.

Hmmm… You know what? That might not be a bad idea. If it worked for others, it might work for me, too…

So let's do it!

Drumroll please…

I will predict the price of… let's say oil… for the next 5 years.

Now, this is very demanding challenge. Let me look into my mystic crystal ball that I always keep in my closet. Yes, yes! I see it! I can see more than one path that the future can carve. Make sure to take some notes…

The first scenario that I can see is the price going up. Yes, that's it! There you have the first scenario.

Now, the second scenario. This one is a little fuzzy. But yes, now it's getting clearer! In the second scenario, the price will go down! Oh my god! Did you expect that? I certainly didn't. What a surprise!

And now there is a third scenario. This one is less likely, but still I can see it in the future. So the third scenario is that the price will stay the same.

But wait!!!

Something else is going on in my crystal ball now. I can also see another scenario! There is a big spaceship. And it's firing a huge laser beam directly towards Earth. Looks like the aliens want to make their new hyperspace bypass, and Earth is in their way.

In that case, we won't care what the price of oil will be.

Let me summarize: the fourth Dark Force of Investing is the fortune-telling investing gurus, who give us a false sense of security about where to invest our money. We may think that they have predictive powers but sadly they don't.

Let me end this segment with a warning. Even after all the proof that the predicting abilities of gurus and other domestic or wild animals are zero, I still get a lot of emails asking me what will happen to the price of stocks, gold, some cryptocurrencies and other assets in the next year. And I bet that after this book is published, I will still receive emails like this one:

*"Robert, I read your book and I really liked the segment about the predicting abilities of investing gurus. I know that gurus cannot predict what will happen, but still...can you tell me what you think will happen to the price of _____ (insert your favorite asset here) in the next year?"*

Some people just don't get it. The only two things that are certain in this world are death and taxes!

## Dark Force #5: Using the Wrong ROI Calculation

This next one is a super important one. I have seen many lives ruined because people didn't know about it. And on top of it all, hardly anybody even talks about it in the investing world.

You are probably familiar with the term Return on Investment (ROI). ROI is probably the most important metric in the investing world. In simple terms, ROI measures how much money was made on the investment as a percentage of the purchase price.

For example, let's say that you invested $1,000 in the shares of ABC company. After awhile, the price of the stock went up and you were able to sell the shares for $1,150.

What was your ROI in that case?

To calculate ROI, the return of your investment needs to be divided by your initial investment. After that you just multiply the result by 100 to get a percentage.

$$ROI = \frac{RETURN}{INITIAL\ INVESTMENT} \times 100$$

So in this case $150 divided by $1,000 equals 0.15. And multiplied by 100 equals 15.

Your ROI, in this case, is 15%.

Simple and easy. No secrets there. Every investing book and website will tell you that.

But what if I told you that the ROI calculation is wrong and misleading?

You might think that I've gone nuts.

But give me a moment to explain what I mean. At one of the seminars I attended at the start of my investing career, one of the speakers was selling a stock-trading course. His claims about the ROI we would get with his trading system were bold, but he made it look so easy, so I started to believe him. And even though he charged almost $2,500 for the ticket, I bought it.

Now, I won't tell you the embarrassing part of this story, where I lost a lot of money and almost had a nervous breakdown as a result of attending the course. To save myself the embarrassment, I will use an average Joe as an example.

When the average Joe attends this kind of course, the first thing he finds out is that you need to have special software in order to use the strategies covered in the course. Ok, that's $450 per month, but who cares about that? Isn't financial freedom worth $450 per month?

Now, the second thing Joe notices is that you need to analyze a lot of stocks with the software every day. So he ends up sitting in front of the computer screen for two hours a day, watching boring charts. But as you know, Joe's goal is financial freedom and isn't Joe's financial freedom worth a couple of hours per day?

After a couple of years of learning and trying, Joe is an experienced trader. And even though he lost some money in the first two years, he has finally become profitable in the third year!

He started the year with $20,000 in his account and now he has $24,000. That's 20% ROI and he is ecstatic. He jumps around the house; he tells all his friends about his achievements. Life couldn't be better! But think again.

Don't you have a strange feeling that we forgot about something when doing the ROI calculation?

Of course! You guessed it. There is his initial investment in the course and there is the monthly cost of the software.

You are right. But I think there is another cost that we didn't account for, and it is much greater than the other two.

It's Joe's time.

And there you have it. ROI calculation is misleading and incomplete if you don't account for the time you spend making and managing your investments.

If you spend 10 hours per week for investing, it is a cost. And from my experience, almost nobody accounts for that when they are calculating their ROI.

So what does the real ROI calculation look like?

$$ROI = \frac{RETURN - COST\ of\ TIME}{INITIAL\ INVESTMENT} \times 100$$

And that makes investing a totally different ball game!

All of a sudden, you realize that if you spend a lot of time investing, your real ROI is much lower than you thought.

But to calculate the real ROI, we need to know what the value of Joe's time is. You can calculate the value of your time by dividing your personal income by the number of hours worked per year. When you calculate this, you get the value of one hour of your time. Try it out for yourself!

$$VALUE\ of\ TIME = \frac{PERSONAL\ INCOME}{HOURS\ WORKED\ PER\ YEAR}$$

Let's say that Joe's annual personal income is $50,000. And let's assume that Joe works 1,800 hours per year (U.S. average according to OEDC)[6].

If we divide $50,000 by 1,800 hours, we get the value of one hour of Joe's time. In this case it's approximately $28 per hour.

If Joe spends 2 hours per day on investing, 200 days per year, that means that he spends 400 hours per year investing.

## 2 HOURS PER DAY X 200 DAYS = 400 HOURS

Let's multiply that by the value of his time ($28 per hour) and we get $11,200. That is the value of the time Joe spent investing in one year.

$$400 \text{ HOURS} \times \$28 \text{ PER HOUR} = \$11,200$$

Now, let's put that into the real ROI equation. First we need to deduct the value of the time Joe spent on investing from his return:

$$\$4,000 - \$11,200 = -\$7,200$$

And now we can finalize the equation by dividing that negative number by $20,000.

$$\frac{-\$7,200}{\$20,000} \times 100 = -36\%$$

That means that the real return is minus 36%.

Joe thought that he made a nice 20% return on investment – but, in reality, he lost 36%.

In the time Joe spent on investing, he could have made money working part-time or setting up a new business. Even flipping hamburgers at McDonalds would have brought in more money than what he did investing!

The fifth Dark Force of Investing is using the wrong ROI calculation. When you account for the time you need to make and manage your investments, your returns often turn negative. That is why not accounting for the cost of time is one of the biggest mistakes I see in the investing world.

## *Dark Force #6: The Lure of the Shiny Next Big Thing*

"If you had purchased $100 of Bitcoins in 2011 you would have more than $200,000 today."

"If you had purchased $1,000 worth of Apple stock in 2003, they would be worth $1 million today."

"If you had ..."

I hear these kinds of claims all the time – in the media, at seminars, in books and on social media. The most disturbing fact is that there are some really smart people, who should know better, making them.

Now, you can't argue against these claims. They are all 100% true. The problem with them is that they are misleading and are responsible for many ruined financial lives.

The goal of making this kind of claim is to convince people that you know what the next big thing is. So a part of the sales presentation where they ask you to invest in a new cryptocurrency (or any other opportunity) will go like this:

"If you had purchased $100 of Bitcoins in 2011, you would have more than $200,000 now. Our new Magic Returns cryptocurrency is next! A small investment of $1,000 could be worth $50,000 in a couple of years, and, if you invest $5,000, you could pay off your entire mortgage!"

Think about it. When somebody is making a claim like that, isn't he or she using just a bit of cherry picking? Ask yourself: how many companies in distress (like Apple) were there in 2003, but didn't make it big, or worse yet, failed in the end?

And how many other cryptocurrencies were there, apart from Bitcoin, that just disappeared?

The answer is hundreds or even thousands, and they all looked the same. So, the probability of choosing the right one was insignificant. Much less than 1%.

When people hear this kind of claim, they often fall prey to the logic error called "survivorship bias." In the investing world, this is the tendency for failed companies to be excluded from performance studies due to the fact that they no longer exist. In other words, you focus only on survivors and you ignore all the failed companies. That is why survivorship bias can lead to overly optimistic beliefs.

When somebody is making claims like, "If you had purchased…," he or she is intentionally misleading people into believing that they can pick the next big winner. In other words, it's a dirty sales technique. Fortunately, you are now immune to this error, because you have read this chapter. Unfortunately, many people have fallen for it.

Investors who read and hear these kinds of claims all the time can get a feeling that it's normal, and quite probable, to get very high returns on their investments. That is why they try to invest in all kinds of legal and illegal investment opportunities where the seller is claiming that very high returns are possible and even highly probable. And, in most cases, they lose their money.

So the sixth Dark Force of Investing is the lure of the shiny next big thing. People often fall prey to survivorship bias and start underestimating the risks involved with any opportunity that offers high potential awards. They try to catch the next big thing and they lose their money in the end.

If I summarize, before you invest your next dime, pay attention to the Six Dark Forces of Investing. They are out there, trying to get you. So, run away as fast as you can when you spot one.

**Exhibit 2.7** The Six Dark Forces of Investing

THE COMMISSION
CAMOUFLAGE EFFECT

REWARD CORRUPTION

BAD GUYS SETTING
THE RULES OF THE GAME

FORTUNE-TELLING
INVESTING GURUS

USING THE WRONG
ROI CALCULATION

THE LURE OF THE
SHINY NEXT BIG THING

Now that you are familiar with the *Six Dark Forces of Investing* that prevent you from getting good returns, or even make you lose a lot of money when investing, you are probably asking yourself how to invest successfully.

In the next chapters I will show you exactly how to do it. We will start with the part where most people make the wrong turn right at the beginning of their investing career. And, when they make that mistake, their dreams about financial success in life are basically over - right away.

Be sure not to make the same mistake. Join me in the next chapter!

## *The Million Dollar Action Plan*

- Time for some digging in your filing cabinet. Check the commissions and fees you are currently paying for the financial products you own. To make a change for the better, you first need to know where you stand!

- Help make this world a better place by sharing the "I'm not R2-D2!" message about the devastating effects of small commissions on your pension pot. My designer prepared a great explainer video that you can share on social media right away. Your friends will love it! You can get it at www.MillionDollarDecisionBook.com/share

*"You must unlearn what you have learned."*

– Master Yoda

# Chapter 3

## Financial Success Formula: How Most People Get It All Wrong?

Success in life is all about making a couple of wise decisions.

My financial downfall was mainly caused by some destructive decisions I made. I made them because of my way of thinking about investing at that time. And our way of thinking always dictates our choices and our actions.

I can say that I had a damaging philosophy about investing and managing my money.

Philosophy is a very powerful word. Webster's Dictionary defines it as a theory or attitude that acts as a guiding principle for behavior.

If you have an incorrect or destructive philosophy in any area of your life, you are basically doomed in that area. For example, if you start your business thinking that it will be easy to succeed, that you don't need to work hard, that you have no competition and so on, you are almost certainly on your way to business failure.

How do you develop a certain philosophy or way of thinking in life? Your parents, peer group, friends, media and other sources of information mainly influence your philosophy. If certain types of information surround you, then you automatically start to believe them and act accordingly.

The fact that I was exposed to a damaging way of thinking about investing at the start of my investing career, cost me a lot of money and time. In retrospect, at that time I was mainly influenced by self-serving financial advisers, bad financial books, deceptive financial websites, misleading financial seminars and corrupt financial companies.

And now the kicker: most people are exposed to the same things. That is why most people have the same damaging philosophy about investing. And that philosophy serves only one party - the financial industry.

When people have this kind of damaging philosophy about investing, it's very easy to take their money. As easy as taking candy from a baby.

Don't be that baby. It's time to unlearn what you have learned about investing.

## *The Investing Philosophy that can Easily Save Your Financial Life*

David is one of the first clients from the UK who attended my workshops. I can still remember the look on his face when he approached me after the workshop and said, "Now I get it! When these financial blokes tell me to do something, the smartest thing I can do is to do the opposite."

"That's a very good way to put it," I replied, laughing.

David's story is a sad one. He spent a fortune learning "the most profitable" investing strategies, and all he had to show for it was huge losses on his investing accounts and a great deal of financial worries.

When we parted, he said to me that the most valuable idea he got from my seminar was not one of the things that I emphasized the most, but something that I just mentioned in a couple of sentences. At that time, I was really surprised to hear that, but when more and more clients mentioned the same thing in their feedback, I decided to teach it in a more structured way.

When I talk about this topic at my seminars, I can always see that people's eyes start to shine and that something transformational happens in their minds. Maybe you will also start to think quite differently about personal finance after you read this chapter.

I'm talking about the Financial Success Formula™. This formula is probably the most important wealth-building philosophy you can adopt. It's the key to your financial success, and everything I teach my kids about money revolves around this philosophy.

So here it is, the Financial Success Formula™:

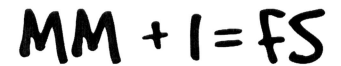

Let me translate it. Money Making (MM) skills plus Investing (I) skills equals Financial Success (FS).

This sounds quite simplistic but bear with me.

If you want to be financially successful, you need to do two things. You need to be able to Make Money – unless you were born with a silver spoon in your mouth. And then you need to know how to Invest a part of that money.

The key word in this formula is AND. If you are good only at one thing, it's not enough.

Let me give you a famous example. Mike Tyson.

Mike Tyson was exceptional at making money. Throughout his boxing career, he made $300 million. This could buy you 1,457 Lamborghini Gallardos, or 40 luxury villas in California.

If you're like most people, you might think that with all that money, you are set for life and you could live happily ever after. There is no way that you could ever have financial problems.

But that was not the case for Mike Tyson. His wild lifestyle and preposterous spending sprees (110 luxury cars, three Bengal tigers and a $2 million bathtub are really essentials to live a happy life) led to him filing for bankruptcy in 2003[7].

This is an extract of an interview Tyson had with The View in 2010[8]:

"I'm totally destitute and broke," Tyson said.

"How did that happen?" asked Joy Behar.

"I had a lot of fun. It just happened," he responded.

Well … it didn't actually just happen. The truth is that Tyson was not financially literate. He simply did not control his money, and he did not understand that he needed to invest part of the money he made. He did not understand that no matter how much you earn, your money simply cannot help you if you do not know how to keep it, how to manage it and invest it. Mike Tyson was great at Making Money but terrible at Investing.

Let me repeat; you need to take care of both sides of this equation to be financially successful. You need to have Money Making AND Investing skills to win the financial game of life. That is the first rule.

But even that is not enough. Even though a lot of people try to take care of both parts, they unfortunately do it in the completely wrong way. That makes them Financial Failures. Let's see how that happens and how to avoid that.

## *This is What Makes Financial Failures*

There are two types of people in this world. Those who are financially successful and those who aren't, and their approaches to this formula are completely different.

First, let's take a look at people who are not financially successful (most people) and ask ourselves, what makes a person a Financial Failure?

A while ago, I met one of my high school friends, and we talked for a while. It was very interesting to listen to his philosophy about money. He told me that he had a corporate job where he made a "lousy" income with no prospects of promotion. He wanted to buy a new car, so he started to invest in binary options (a very risky short-term trading strategy, similar to gambling). I tried to convince him that the only people making money with binary options were brokers, and then I asked him why didn't he learn some business skills and start a home-based business in his spare time instead of that.

His answer was: "I thought about that, but it's too risky."

My friend had the classical Financial Failure type of thinking. While he didn't want to "risk" improving his Money Making skills, he had no trouble gambling his money away with binary options.

Go figure.

A person who is a Financial Failure is not aggressive enough in the Money Making part of the formula. He is scared to death of starting a part-time business. He is not taking wise, calculated risks. He's always on the safe side. If he tries a new Money Making activity, he quickly gives up after the first obstacles. Instead of learning new Money Making skills, he is watching the news on TV, or gossiping with his friends. That is why he never even gets the chance to notably increase his income.

Then we come to the 'I' side of the equation - Investing. The same person who was scared to death to start a new business, or to take some calculated risks in the Money Making part of the formula, becomes a risk-taking maniac in the Investing part of the formula.

He starts to gamble with his money and make uneducated decisions. Neighbors tell him there is an opportunity to get a 30% guaranteed return from some obscure investment opportunity and he takes it. He starts to trade stocks or currencies for a quick profit and jumps on the binary options trading wagon while hoping to get rich quick. He spends hours per day sitting in front of his computer watching the charts.

Then the inevitable happens. He loses his money because his neighbor's opportunity was a Ponzi scheme and short-term trading is a losing game from the start. So, instead of getting rich quick, he loses most, or even all, of his invested money. On top of that, he spends a lot of time doing it. Time that could be better spent learning new Money Making skills.

## *Turn Things Around for Financial Success*

Now that we know what kind of behavior leads to becoming a Financial Failure, let's find out what it takes to be financially successful. To illustrate this, let me take you back to one of the most important moments of my life.

If you were with me in the winter of 2004, you would be looking at me and my girlfriend Sara, in our tiny 450 square foot apartment we had just rented. We don't have enough money to buy a bed yet, so the mattress on the floor is our only solution.

It's a dark, rainy day outside. The furniture in the apartment is old and worn-down, the lights are dim, not really the place you dream of spending the rest of your life.

You see us talking with concerned looks on our faces. The tension is thick enough to be felt. It's the kind of tension you feel when you need to make a decision, which you really don't want to make. A decision that could change the course of your life or ruin you.

"Robert, do you realize that we have everything riding on this? If this doesn't go as planned, if we don't fill the room, if his flight is delayed or if something else that we can't control happens, we'll go bankrupt, we'll be ruined!"

"Yeah, I know, Sara," I replied quietly, thinking about what that would mean for us. The company we founded in a student dorm three years before that was just able to break even. If we didn't nail this seminar we would be in debt for years to come.

And then I slowly continued, "And I am also aware that we don't have enough money to do it. It would be better to wait a couple of years until we are an established company, and I also know that I don't have a good idea of how we will promote it."

"... But it's a unique opportunity - it's once in a lifetime chance to do something incredible. We have to take the risk."

So, we decided to go for it – to organize our first big seminar with the legendary public speaker and author Brian Tracy.

We had a lot of difficulty raising enough money; we were scared. But we gave it our best, and the rest is history. The conference hall was full, the clients were very happy, we earned a lot of money and became friends and business partners with Brian.

It would have been very easy to find excuses to not do this project. We did not have the money, it was clearly very risky, our company was still on shaky ground, and we were way too young...

Unsuccessful people in life have a lot of opportunities to achieve their goals and dreams, but they avoid the risk. They don't venture into the waters and stay safely on the shore, and they avoid anything that might make them uncomfortable.

Successful people know that in order to succeed in Money Making activities, you need to take calculated risks; that you need to be assertive. Just a "safe" job will never solve your financial problems.

If you avoid risk, you will never grab the key opportunities in life.

And this is one of the biggest mistakes people make in their financial lives.

The Financial Success Formula™ for financially successful people looks like this:

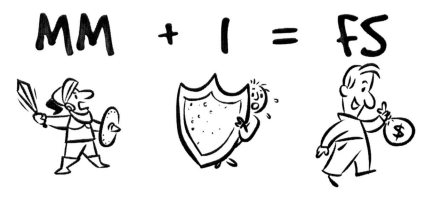

When it comes to their Money Making activities, they are very assertive! They learn new skills that allow them to make more money. They are building their personal brands. They take calculated risks. If they fail, they get up and try again and again until they succeed. In other words, they draw their swords and attack until the battle is done.

As for the Investing part of the equation, they are very cautious and conservative. They know that they need to invest to make their money work for them, but they only invest in opportunities that they understand. They don't try to beat the market with wild, short-term trading. They don't make costly mistakes; they don't fall prey to financial predators and Ponzi schemes. And, most important of all:

they don't spend a lot of time investing. They understand that passive, long-term investing works much better than short-term gambling with their money.

This enables them to feel financially secure and confident about their financial life, with far-reaching consequences. Think about it: if you are not investing, if your net worth is zero, or even in the negative territory, this will affect you even if you think it won't! It will affect how you see yourself, how confident you are, how you think and, ultimately, how you act.

Our mind is a very simple mechanism. If it sees proof of something, it will believe it's true. If it doesn't, then all the positive thinking and visualizations in the world will not help you.

## "The definition of a person who practices visualization and positive thinking, without taking action: a broke loser."

**@RobertRolih #MillionDollarDecision**

Your mind needs to see the raw reality - the reality where you are wisely managing your money and investing it, and not just thinking about it.

"Someday" will not cut it! If you are not already, you need to start investing right away, to give your mind proof that something is going in the right direction. When your brain sees the new reality, the snowball effect kicks in, and you will start to make and invest more money.

Let me summarize: most people are very cautious when they need to make more money. They are afraid to start a new business; they are not assertive enough; they are not prepared to learn the business skills needed.

But, if you want to be financially successful, you need to be aggressive and risk taking with Making Money and very careful and passive when you are investing it. Being passive in the Investing part of the equation saves you a lot of time that you can channel into your Money Making activities and thus make more money.

I cannot emphasize that concept enough. This is the key concept you should use in your life, if you want to be a financially well off when you are still young enough to enjoy it!

## *The Great Misconception About Investing*

One of the reasons why people mess up the Financial Success Formula™ is the big misconception about what investing really is. A lot of people think that they are Investing their money, but, in reality, they are conducting Money Making activities.

That is why it is imperative that we draw a clear line between Money Making and Investing. Here is my simple definition that will help us do that.

Money Making activities are activities where you put in your **time** and **sometimes money** in order to make money. Investing is the activity where you buy an investment, and then your **money works for you passively** – without you lifting a finger. When you are investing, you buy an asset and this asset hopefully generates an income or appreciates in the future. The key aspect of Investing is that there is no additional work needed after you have bought an asset.

**Exhibit 3.1** The definition of Money Making and Investing

YOU WORKING FOR MONEY          MONEY PRODUCING MORE MONEY

Now, let's play a quiz and try to put a clear line between different Money Making and Investing activities.

## Your Own Business

When you are thinking about how to increase your income, one of the first and probably best options that comes to mind is starting a business.

We all know that running your own business can be very profitable. After all, there are millions of people all around the world who got rich with their business. But make no mistake - running your own business is a time-consuming activity. If you want to be successful in business, you will need to work hard. I'm a business owner, and I personally know hundreds of business owners with whom I cooperate. They all worked hard to be successful. No exceptions. There is no way around it.

My late friend Chet Holmes, who was a top marketing consultant, once said that a lot of people start their business to have more free time. Then he added that this is like planning to have kids and thinking that you will have more free time after that.

There are some people who claim that they will show you how to set up a business that runs passively, but believing that is, unfortunately, just like believing in Santa. After you attend their courses, you realize that setting up a passive business model will take you years of hard work. That's hardly passive, in my opinion.

After that, you need to take into account that the world is changing rapidly. So, even if you set up a somewhat passive business structure, it will need adjustments. There will be new competitors you need to fight, new marketing channels you need to use, new customer needs you need to satisfy. And that takes time.

## "Passive business models are mostly the stuff of fairy tales."

**@RobertRolih #MillionDollarDecision**

My verdict: running your own business is a time-consuming Money Making activity. Probably one of the best ones. More millionaires were created through business than through any other Money Making activity.

### Real Estate Investing

Investing in real estate has become increasingly popular over the last decades. The model is pretty simple on the surface. There are two ways you can make money in real estate. The first one is to buy a property, hope that it appreciates in value and then sell it. The second model is that you buy a property and rent it out to a tenant where the rent you collect is equal or higher than the mortgage plus all the other costs and taxes.

When I ask people who attend my seminars if investing in real estate falls under Money Making or Investing, most of them say that it's Investing. Right?

Wrong!

When we think about investing in real estate, we have this illusion that we will buy a house or some apartments, get tenants in no time and then just collect the rent for years and years. To complete the illusion, we could say, when we have 10 houses we can live happily ever after, with tons of passive income coming in every month.

Is this what really happens? Not by a long shot.

Real estate investing is just another type of business, and even though some people think it's passive, it's not. It's a very time-consuming Money Making activity. You need to go through thousands of listings, you need to select the ones that fit your criteria, you need to see the properties, you need to negotiate the price, you need to manage the property, you have legal problems when the tenants don't pay the rent. You have to spend time or money keeping it in good shape. You need to work hard to get a good return on an investment in the real estate business.

Am I saying that real estate investing is not a good business model? No, of course not. Many people have gotten rich by investing in real estate. I'm just saying it's not passive. It's not a type of investment where you just put in some money, and it works for you passively. Real estate is just like any other kind of business. It has its specifics that you might like or not. If you like that type of business, go ahead, but don't think that you will not need to work hard to succeed. It's a far cry from checking some listings, buying a house, getting some tenants and enjoying the windfall of passive income.

You have probably heard many real estate experts say that we should all invest in real estate. But this is like saying that we should all own hairdressing salons.

Now you are probably thinking, "But what about outsourcing the property management and other services?"

Yes, in your real estate business, you can hire people and outsource a lot of things, just as in any other type of business. But this doesn't mean that you can do that from the start. In business, you first need to work hard for years to be successful, and then you can automate and outsource some activities, or hire people to do them. You just can't outsource running a business, at least not from the start.

My verdict: Investing in real estate is a Money Making activity. It's just like running any other type of business. So, a better name for it would be a "real estate business."

## Stocks

You probably guessed right. Yes, investing in stocks and stock funds (stock funds are a basket of stocks) falls under Investing. Why? Because after you have bought a stock, there is nothing you need to do in order for it to produce returns.

For example, if you buy one Apple stock, you become a shareholder of Apple. A stock is simply a share in the ownership of a company. People in the financial industry use different names for it, like shares, stocks or equities. But they basically all mean the same thing.

When you own a company's stock, it means that you have a claim to everything the company owns – brands, offices and patents. That claim is, of course, a very small one, because you own a very small percentage of the company. The important part of being an owner of the company is that you are entitled to your share of the company's earnings. So, when the company is profitable and decides to distribute a portion of its earnings, you receive a small part of it. This is called a dividend.

So if you buy an Apple stock today, you are hoping that:

1. Apple stock price will go up in time, and you will profit from the rise in stock price.

2. That the company will be profitable in the future and will pay out dividends.

And the best thing is that for getting both benefits, you don't need to lift a finger after you have bought the stock.

Pretty straightforward, don't you think? At least if you are investing for the long run; and I define long run as investing for at least 10 years or more.

What about trading stocks in the short run? There are many people who try to profit from short-term price swings. They may own a stock for a couple of hours, days, weeks or months. These people are called speculators. When they speculate and trade stocks all the time, they are spending their time and energy. That makes trading stocks a Money Making activity, and, usually, a very risky one.

My verdict: Investing in stocks is an Investing activity if you invest for the long run and a Money Making activity if you speculate and trade stocks for the short run.

## Bonds

This is an easy one. Bonds fall under Investing.

If you are not familiar with bonds, here is a simple explanation. Bonds are a fixed-income security. That means that the interest you get is fixed; for example, 2% annually. That is similar to bank deposits, but bank deposits have lower interest rates.

Governments and corporations in need of fresh money usually issue bonds. For example, the U.S. or any other government finds out that it doesn't have enough money to finance all the expenditures it faces. In other words, the money coming in is not enough to cover all expenses, such as social security, education, science, military, etc.

So, the government needs to find a way to get some additional money in the budget to balance it. One of the most common ways is to borrow that money through the issue of bonds. Individuals, companies, pension plans, foundations and other countries can buy these bonds.

When you buy a government bond, you are effectively lending some money to the government so it can pay its bills. In exchange for that, the government awards you with interest (a coupon) and returns the principal (your initial investment) at the end of the loan period (maturity date).

Here is a simplified example: you buy a bond that has a 2% interest rate, and a ten-year maturity date, for $1,000. So, for the next 10 years, you will receive $20 (2%) annually, and after ten years, you will get back your initial investment of $1,000.

If we compare stocks and bonds we can quickly see that the main difference for the investor is that bonds offer you lower, but fixed and guaranteed, returns. Stocks on the other hand, normally have much higher returns in the long run, but their short-term, year-to-year returns can be very volatile.

My verdict: Investing in bonds is, of course, an Investing activity.

## Forex, Options, Binary Options

Trading currencies, commodities, options, binary options and all sorts of other short-term instruments is all the rage right now. That is why we will go into more detail in chapter 6. But, for now, let's just establish if trading with these instruments is a Money Making or Investing activity.

The aim of short-term trading is simple. You want to buy a currency, or any other instrument, at one price and sell it at a higher price in order to make a profit (you can also make money by selling at one price and buying it at a lower price, but let's not get too technical here).

The brokers who offer this kind of trading usually refer to it as Investing, but it's a far cry from that. It's a time-consuming speculation.

In short: it's a Money Making activity. But because the odds of losing your money are so high, we could easily say that it's a **money losing pursuit**, and not Money Making.

For example, when you trade currencies (Forex or Foreign Exchange market), you are basically trying to guess which way a certain currency pair will move in the short run. It's a lot like gambling. Very risky, and you need a lot of time and wasted money before you even have the smallest chance of winning. The same goes for all the other short-term trading instruments.

# "Love risk when making money. Hate risk when investing money."

### @RobertRolih #MillionDollarDecision

In the last couple of years, I have constantly received a lot of questions regarding binary options, probably because they are so heavily advertised online. So let me explain what they are. Binary options are a cunning gambling instrument that gives you a feeling that the odds of winning are on your side. But in reality, the house (the broker) has an enormous edge that makes this gambling game almost impossible to win. When you are trading binary options, you are betting if a certain stock or currency will go up or down in a certain period of time. Of course, the odds of winning would be exactly 50:50, if there were no commissions. But the high commissions eat your money up making this a losing game from the start.

My verdict: trading Forex, or any other short-term instrument, is a Money Making activity - usually a very risky one with a very low probability of actually making money. When I refer to the Money

Making activities in this book from now on, I will do so with a premise that short-term trading or speculating is **not included** in them.

## Precious Metals

There are a lot of precious metals in which you can invest, but, for most investors, gold and silver are the only viable options, because they are very simple to buy and own.

When you invest in precious metals, you need to understand that, unlike stocks, they don't pay out dividends. So, when you invest in gold and silver, you are only hoping that the price will go up in time. This may happen, but it can also go down.

The prices of precious metals are influenced by a lot of factors we cannot predict, like interest rates, the state of the global economy, inflation, supply and demand, etc. That is why it's very hard to predict where the price of a certain precious metal will be in 5, 10 or 20 years. For example, if you bought gold in 1980, you would only see negative returns on your investment for 20 years or so.

My verdict: Investing in precious metals is an Investing activity if you invest for the long run and a Money Making activity if you speculate and trade precious metals in the short run.

**Exhibit 3.2** Drawing a line between Money Making and Investing

**MM**

- BUSINESS
- REAL ESTATE
- ANY SHORT-TRADING OR SPECULATION

**I**

- STOCKS
- BONDS
- PRECIOUS METALS
- BANK DEPOSITS

## *Get Rich by Combining Both Parts of the Formula*

So how do you make the Financial Success Formula work for you?

We have already established that you need to be assertive in the Money Making part of the formula, and very careful in the Investing part of the formula. You should spend the lion's share of your time in the Money Making part of the formula, including learning new Money Making and business skills, building your personal brand and, if you haven't already, maybe even start your own business. Then, spending as little time as possible in the Investing part of the formula. As you will see later in the book, people who try to make Investing a Money Making activity, through short-term speculations, usually end up broke.

Spending more time in the Money Making part of the formula allows you to increase your income. The more income you have, the more money you can invest to work passively for you. This gives you additional financial security and, in time, can make you truly financially free.

**Exhibit 3.3** Investing a part of your profits

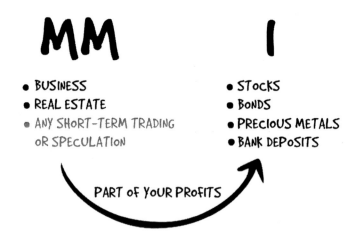

72

Let's face it. It's very hard to become rich by investing alone. If you try to force high returns with short-term speculation, you usually lose both your money and your time. If you invest small sums of money the smart way, it takes a lot of time to become rich.

If you are like me, then the prospect of becoming rich when you are 75 years old is not a nice prospect. You probably want to become rich while you can still enjoy it. That is why you need to improve your Money Making skills to be able to make more money and to invest more. When you invest larger amounts of money, the investing game becomes really enjoyable and very profitable.

Let's check some scenarios!

If you invest $3,000 annually, and you are lucky enough to get a 10% average return in the future (10% is the average annual historical return for stocks, which may or may not continue in the future), you will need 36 years to become a millionaire. Now, don't get me wrong – this is still much better than spending all of your money every month, but 36 years is a long period of time.

If you increase your income and you don't spend the increase on unnecessary things, this can allow you to invest $10,000 annually. With a 10% average annual return, you will need 25 years to become a millionaire.

If you further increase your income and you invest $30,000 annually, you will only need 15 years to become a millionaire.

And if you are successful in any business that could even allow you to invest $100,000 annually. This makes you a millionaire in 6.5 years. Now, that is something to look forward to!

**Exhibit 3.4** Time needed to become a millionaire

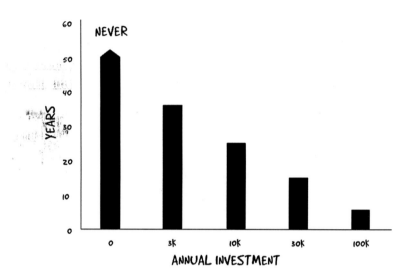

In my opinion, the best way to make a lot of money is by owning a business. Starting a business is not for everyone. If you want to be successful in business, you need to learn the proper business skills, like marketing and selling. But running a successful business can exponentially increase your income. Compared to a job where your income is limited, or can grow very slowly, in running your own business, your income can grow fast. There are no limits to how much money you can make.

But even if you run a successful business and you make a lot of money, it's smart to put a part of that money into passive investments. Why?

A lot of business owners say that the best and the safest investment is to invest in their company, and, for the most part, I agree. The best investment you can make in the first years of your company's operation is in your own business. But let's face it – it's far from the safest. Anybody's business can get into trouble. There can be a huge shift in the marketplace, crisis, big competitors entering the market, or you can have an accident. There are thousands of things that can happen to any business to make it a bust.

The U.S. Bureau of Labor Statistics says that about half of all new businesses don't survive five years or more[9]. So even if you think (and I'm sure you do) that failure can't happen to your business, it's better to be on the safe side.

That is why I'm actively encouraging people to invest in their businesses. In the first years, you can invest almost all of your money into your business, but as you start to make some money, start increasing the amounts you invest in passive investments.

Putting all of your eggs in one basket – your business – can be dangerous. One of my clients, a successful business owner, created a very profitable company and lost it because he had a car accident and was not able to work for more than a year. He lost all of his money because he invested everything he had into his own business. If he had put a part of his business profits into passive investments, he would have financially survived the accident, but unfortunately, he didn't.

Now, that you are familiar with the Financial Success Formula™, we can move on to the next step. But contrary to what you might think, the next step is not about investing your money. Before we start to invest money, we need to take care of something even more important. You will find out what that is in the next chapter.

## *The Million Dollar Action Plan*

- Apply the Financial Success Formula™ in your life and teach your children about it. This philosophy can have a profound effect on their life.

- If you want to invest more, you first need to make more money. If you would like to increase your income, check out the bonus resources at www.MillionDollarDecisionBook.com/bonus. When you register, you will also start to receive my *Million Dollar Strategies Newsletter*, where I share my best strategies and tactics for increasing your income.

*"Expect the best, plan for the worst and prepare to be surprised."*

– Denis Waitley

# Chapter 4

## Just Don't Sign Here: The Perils of Financial Safety?

**O**ne strike and you are out.

In medieval times, swords were the weapons of choice for most duels and battlefield encounters. When men prepared and trained themselves for fights, they focused first on the defense tactics. Once they were proficient at defense, they went on to practice offensive tactics.

Why is that?

Because if you can't defend yourself, it only takes one strike from the opponent and you are dead. No defensive skills meant a very short fight and a short life.

It's the same in our financial life. You can use a lot of offensive strategies and tactics to earn more money and to invest it with a goal to get good returns. Like a swordsman needs to attack frequently, so that one of the attacks will hit the mark, the money making initiatives that you employ sometimes work and sometimes they don't. That is why it is essential that you try many of them. Especially in business, you need to try many different tactics to find out what works for your market.

But unfortunately, there are also a lot of dangerous opponents we face in our financial lives. Most of them work undercover and are very hard to detect before it's too late. If you don't prepare some defensive tactics in advance, a single strike can mean game over for you.

That is why one of the most important rules of personal finance is that you take care of the defense first, and only after that should you start to attack. In fact, one of the biggest mistakes people make is that they skip this important step. They start investing to get good returns, without taking care of their financial defense first.

This chapter is all about your defensive strategy.

It will give you a solid foundation on which you can build your wealth without worries. By using the principles in this chapter, you will be able to sleep well at night, because you will know that you are covered in case something bad happens.

## Black Swans: the Most Dangerous Animals

Life is not fair.

Even if you are the kindest, smartest, most generous and most positive person, something totally unforeseen can happen that turns everything around.

People get into accidents. Planes crash. People get cancer. People get hit by lightning. People have a heart attack during yoga class. People get hit in the head by a pigeon when riding a bicycle. And no, I'm not kidding. That really happened to someone.

We live in a world governed by the laws of quantum physics and the key principle in quantum physics says that there is no certainty in this world. There are only probabilities. The harsh reality is that anything can happen, even the so-called "black swan" events.

The term "black swan" originated in 17th century London. At that time, there was a presumption that all swans must be white because only white swans were found until then. That is why people believed that there were no black swans. Or more precisely, they didn't even think about the possibility that black swans to existed, but that changed when Willem de Vlamingh discovered black swans in Australia. The term "black swan" became popular recently because of the book with the same title, written by Nassim Nicholas Taleb.

# "There is no certainty in the world. There are only probabilities."

### @RobertRolih #MillionDollarDecision

In that book, Taleb gives examples of black swan events, like the 9/11 attacks, or the rise of Google[10]. He claims that almost all important events in history come from the unexpected, and I think he is right. Even though, in retrospect, we think that we should be able to predict the 9/11 attacks or the dominance of Google (uh, I should have bought that stock), this is just our human nature at work.

Humans like things that are sequential. We understand the law of cause and effect and that is why we try to explain those kinds of events in such terms. We may even think that we could predict them. The signs and the causes were there.

But the harsh reality is that we couldn't predict the 9/11 attacks. You couldn't predict Google's success. You couldn't predict the key events that made you who you are. There were no signs.

We live in a world governed by uncertainty and chance. Probably the only way to be really certain about your life is to build an underground bunker, get a lifetime supply of food, seal it off and live there happily ever after (don't forget a huge supply of books and movies). And even then, you could stumble on your way to the toilet and get hit in the head by a low-hanging beam.

In short, life is a risky business and you can never eliminate all the risks; but you can prepare for some common ones, and take care of some of your safety needs.

Hopefully, you are familiar with Abraham Maslow's Hierarchy of Needs model[11]. If not, that's ok. We will go over it here. Even though there were a lot of updates to this model in the last decades, our understanding of human motivation can still be described quite well with this model. Maslow said that there are five basic levels of human needs:

1. Biological and Physiological needs - air, food, drink, shelter, warmth, sex, sleep, etc.

2.  Safety needs - protection from the elements, security, order, law, stability, etc.

3.  Belongingness and Love needs - family, work group, affection, relationships, etc.

4.  Esteem needs - self-esteem, achievement, mastery, independence, status, dominance, prestige, etc.

5.  Self-actualization needs - realizing personal potential, self-fulfillment, seeking personal growth.

The key point of the model is that a person must satisfy his/her lower level basic needs before progressing on to meet higher level growth needs. Once these needs have been satisfied, a person may be able to reach the highest level, called self-actualization.

As you can see, safety needs are the second level in this model. So, after we have enough food and a secure shelter, we look for safety.

Safety needs have changed a lot throughout history because of the different dangers lurking for us out there. In the past, you could get eaten by a lion, beheaded in the revolution, taken into slavery or attacked by a wild bunch of cowboys. But in today's developed world, we think about our safety mostly in the following ways:

*   What if I lose my job?
*   What if my business goes south?
*   What if I have an accident and I'm disabled?
*   What if something happens to my significant other?
*   What would happen to my family if I die?
*   What would happen if my house or apartment burns down/gets broken into or gets destroyed in a natural disaster?

Ok, some people also ask themselves more exotic questions like, "what if I'm abducted by aliens" or "what if the world ends?"

Even though these scenarios are certainly possible, they are quite unlikely, and, apart from that, you can't do much about them. So, let's stay with the first set of dangers – the ones where you can do something to protect yourself and your family.

In order to help you, the financial industry created insurance products to protect you, but the problem is that a lot of these products are only designed to pay the insurance company, not protect you. These products seem good, but, in reality, don't provide you the coverage you expected. Also, there are some products that are quite misleading in their advertised claims and are responsible for people losing a lot of money.

Let me remind you: the most aggressively sold financial products are the worst for customers. And insurance products are not an exception.

## *Financial Safety With the A.R.M.O.R. Formula*™

Let's face it. Insurance is boring most of the time. You have to pay premiums every month, and that money vanishes into thin air. The best case scenario is that you never get any of that money back. Because if you did, that would mean that something bad happened to you, your family, or to your property.

Fortunately, most people realize that even though insurance is boring, it's also a must, and it's a must before you need it. When you are buying different products, like a new car, shoes or a computer, you buy them when you need them. Insurance companies, though, will not sell you insurance when you need it. It's too late by then. You need to buy it before something happens, and usually the best time to do it is now.

To help you select the right insurance policies and make sure you don't end up with one of the many bad products, I developed a simple formula that will guide you in this area. I call it the A.R.M.O.R. formula™. This is a formula that will save you thousands of dollars and help you to make sure that you are covered in case something bad happens.

The first thing you need to do when thinking about protecting yourself is to **Assess the Risk Factors.**

# A.R.M.o.R. FoRMULA™

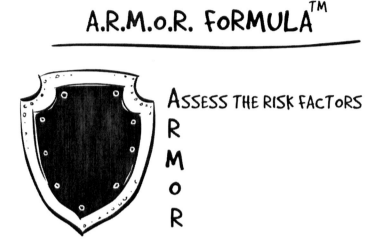

ASSESS THE RISK FACTORS
R
M
o
R

There are a lot of risk factors facing us, and we can never prepare ourselves for all of them, but let's take a look at the most common ones, and analyze the insurance policies that enable you to protect yourself and your family in case they happen.

But before we dive into the specific products, a quick note to non-U.S. readers: even though the next chapters of this book are written with the U.S. reader in mind, the main principles and products are practically the same all over the world. But, of course, there are some important distinctions that you need to be aware of, depending on where you reside. Visit www.MillionDollarDecisionBook.com/bonus for more information on how to get recommendations for your country of residence.

# #1 Losing your ability to work

Today, 25 million American lives are restricted by the effects of a disability, according to the Centers for Disease Control and Prevention. That's a scary statistic. Furthermore, the Social Security Administration estimates that over one in four of today's 20 year-olds will become disabled before reaching age 67[12].

Your ability to earn money is one of the most important assets that you have. If you are disabled, your income is usually drastically reduced. That can seriously jeopardize the financial well-being of your family.

## Insurance policy to have: Long-Term Disability Insurance

Disability insurance provides you with an income should you be disabled and unable to work. The key when choosing a plan is to choose a disability policy that provides enough coverage to enable you to continue your current lifestyle, in case you can no longer work.

If you are traditionally employed, you should be able to secure a policy through your employer, while if you are self-employed, you will have to take out an individual policy. If you can't get enough coverage with your group coverage, you may buy the increased coverage by buying private policies to supplement those from your employer. This is very important if you have a family dependent on your income.

Also, keep in mind that disability insurance companies won't sell you an insurance policy to replace 100% of your income. Usually, they sell policies that go up to about 70% of your current income. If you don't have at least 70% of your current income provided through your employer's disability insurance plan, you should obtain supplemental coverage to bring you up to 70%.

When you are looking for disability insurance, expect that individual policies are more expensive than employer-sponsored coverage. But one of the major advantages of individual disability insurance is that because you pay the premiums, the benefits you receive are tax-free. Tax-free benefits of 70% of your current income may be close to 100% of your current after-tax income. On the other hand, if your employer pays the premium for the insurance coverage, all the benefits you receive are taxable as ordinary income.

## #2 Serious illness

According to U.S. bankruptcy court statistics, more than 1.5 million people file for bankruptcy every year[13]. The no. 1 reason for filing bankruptcy, by far, is medical expenses.

The most interesting fact is that 75% of these bankrupt people had health insurance, but according to the team of researchers at Harvard Law School, they still couldn't pay all their medical bills and debts[14].

For an average middle or upper middle-class American family, health insurance offers inadequate protection. That is why Harvard's Dr. David Himmelstein says that, "Unless you're Warren Buffett, your family is just one serious illness away from bankruptcy."

## Insurance policy to have: Health insurance

Health insurance plans fall into two categories: individual coverage and group coverage. Group plans (employer-sponsored coverage) are provided by an employer or worker's union, and individual plans are negotiated between an individual and the insurance company.

If a group insurance plan is available to you, use it, because it will probably provide more comprehensive coverage than an individual plan. Group insurance pools policies within an organization and can significantly lower the costs for you.

When you use employer-sponsored coverage, your employer may give you a choice of health insurance plans and pay for all or some of your monthly premium.

If you are buying individual insurance, you will need to shop around and choose a plan that covers you and your family. You will also need to know and manage all of your health coverage and benefits. That is why I recommend you to consult with a health plan advisor, because there are a lot of different options from which you need to choose. When you talk to the advisor, ask a lot of "what if" questions in order to choose the right plan for yourself. Also, don't hesitate to ask questions when you don't understand something.

## #3 Car accident

Every year, more than 2 million people in the U.S. alone are injured in traffic crashes[15]. The problem with driving a car is that even if you are a very experienced and careful driver, you can never eliminate the possibility of somebody causing an accident where you are involved.

## Insurance policy to have: Car insurance

Car insurance is required by law, but it pays to check your car insurance carefully because you can have different levels of coverage depending on which insurance policy you purchase. As many people find out, they are underinsured for lawsuits.

The most common limit for medical coverage is $100,000 per person, but that is not even close enough to cover medical bills in a serious accident. It will surprise you that you can increase that limit to $300,000 - $1 million, or more, with a very small increase in cost.

In addition, take into account that many drivers have no insurance or they are underinsured. That is why you should also increase your uninsured and underinsured motorist coverage on your car insurance.

## #4 Losing your life

Losing your life is not so much a problem for you (well, at least not after you have died), but for the people who financially depend on you – your spouse, children, and other loved ones. They could face big financial problems that could ruin their lives if you pass away.

## Insurance policy to have: Life insurance

Life insurance is a must if you have minor children, if you plan to have them, if your family has debts like the mortgage, or if you have a spouse who earns less than you. If you don't have any dependents (and you don't plan to have them in the future), or if you have accumulated enough assets to be financially independent, you don't really need to spend money on life insurance.

There are many different options and types of life insurance policies available. The two basic types of life insurance are whole life insurance and term life insurance.

The main difference between them is that the whole life policies are permanent and have two components: an insurance component and an investment component (usually called a "cash value").

This means that when you buy whole life insurance, a part of the premiums you pay will be invested somewhere (usually in mutual funds, bonds or similar). The monthly premium that you are paying goes into three buckets: the first part goes toward the insurance portion of your policy, the second part goes toward administrative expenses and the balance goes toward the investment (or cash) portion of your policy.

Term life insurance, on the other hand, only has an insurance component. It has no cash value at the end. All the premiums you paid are just a normal cost for you.

At first glance, you would think that whole life insurance is way better than term life insurance, and you would be right, but only if you meant for the insurance companies and their brokers. I will explain this in detail in the next segment.

In my opinion, a term life policy is much better than whole life policy. Term life insurance means that you purchase life insurance that provides coverage at a fixed rate of payments for a limited period of time, usually 15 to 25 years, and is the least expensive way to purchase a substantial death benefit.

For most families, that makes this policy effective until their children move out and become financially independent. Once kids are independent, there is no reason to continue paying for life insurance. The 15 to 25-year period also allows you to build some assets. If you pass away after that, your spouse and children will inherit these assets.

As for the coverage (the benefit your family will get in case you die), I recommend an amount that replaces at least 10 times your annual income. So, if your income is $50,000, the coverage should be at least $500,000.

But you need to be careful when you buy this type of life insurance. The cost of premiums increases almost exponentially with your age. So, if you are thinking about getting one, do it right away. If you wait for just a year or two, the monthly premiums you will need to pay will be much higher.

Term life insurance policies boast many different features, benefits and prices. Shop around carefully, and talk to the agent to be certain that you understand the coverage and the cost. Buying life insurance is a once in a lifetime decision. Don't make it a bad one.

## *Better Safe than Sorry*

When you have assessed the risk factors in your life, and chosen the types of insurance policies you need, it's time to Review insurance companies.

# A.R.M.o.R. FoRMULA™

**ASSESS THE RISK FACTORS**
**REVIEW INSURANCE COMPANIES**
**M**
**o**
**R**

Picking the right insurance company today is easier than ever. The internet has made it very easy to check the customer reviews, credit ratings and other important factors. When selecting the company from whom you will buy insurance, be careful about the following factors:

## The company's reputation

When checking the suitability of an insurance company, the first step is to check the company reviews on the internet. No company will have 100% positive reviews, but always choose the one that has a lot of positive ratings. Check if they provide prompt responses to questions and inquiries and how fast do they solve customers' problems? Then, check out the nature of the problems that unhappy clients had with the insurance company. If you see that the company has problems with non-compensation of its policyholders, that's a red flag.

# "It pays to do a thorough check of the insurance company before you buy insurance."

**@RobertRolih #MillionDollarDecision**

Also, check the Better Business Bureau website (www.bbb.org). There you can see how the company has been operating, the rating of the company and other interesting facts. I tend to buy my insurance policies from companies that have been in business for at least 30 years. When a company has been in business that long, you can be certain that it understands the complexities of the insurance business and how to manage risk. That is, of course, not a guarantee that they will be in business forever, but it's much more likely that the company will survive another 30 years, compared to a startup.

## Does it have a local office?

We are used to buying all sorts of products online now, and, in most cases, it doesn't matter where the company from whom you buy is located. For insurance products, it is better to go with an insurance company that has a physical presence in your area. If things start to go ugly, having a personal one-to-one conversation could be a life saver.

## Terms and price

Insurance companies can offer you quite a range of quotes. To find out which company has the best prices, ask for quotes from at least three reputable insurance companies, and then compare them. If you work with an insurance broker, he or she can help you with that. But don't rely solely on the opinion of your insurance broker.

Keep in mind that their motivation is to sell you the policies where they get the best compensation from the insurance companies. So, they might be tempted to recommend to you the policies that are the best for them and not necessarily the best for you.

## *The Hottest-Selling Insurance: The Greatest Weapon of Financial Self-Destruction*

The next step in the A.R.M.O.R. formula™ is my favorite one.

Back in the days when I didn't have a clue about the topic of personal finance and investing, and I just trusted my financial advisers, I bought one of the best financial products available on the market. Later on, I found out that it was the best one for the adviser and not for me.

Unfortunately, this product is owned by millions of people all around the world, and is one of the top selling financial products. Even though the insurance companies have a different, very sexy name for it, I call it "The Greatest Weapon of Financial Self-Destruction."

The product I talk about has many different names and can be presented differently in different countries. The common names are: whole life insurance, universal life insurance, variable life insurance, equity-indexed annuity and so on.

When you are buying life insurance and you want to spot this type of insurance, look out for this feature: your policy has both an insurance and an investment component (usually called a "cash value.") This means that the seller of these types of policies will tell you that you will have life insurance, plus a part of the premiums you pay will be invested somewhere (usually in mutual funds, bonds or something similar).

When you spot these features in a financial product, there is a very straightforward strategy that you need to follow: run away as fast as possible.

Let me show you how they work and you will be amazed by the cunningness of the financial industry.

Like I said, in the past I owned two policies like that. They were both highly recommended by my financial adviser.

The first one was a whole life policy that I still own, because the penalties for terminating it are just too high, and the second one is my favorite example that shows you the damage that these policies can do.

When I bought it, the advisor told me that because I already have a whole life insurance policy from another company, I should get another one that is even more "investment oriented." That is why the vast majority of the premiums that I pay would go into a global mutual fund, and only a small percentage of the premiums would go towards the life insurance.

In his words, that product was an alternative to investing directly in this global mutual fund, but with some tax advantages. That is why I should get a good and safe return on my investments because my money is being invested in the world economy.

"Sounds nice," I thought, and I started to put around $165 per month into this product, and I was also very lucky – the timing was great.

In the next years, the market went down sharply, to 50% of its value, and my monthly investments bought more and more units of this global mutual fund. This is a good thing - I was buying low!

After three years, the market started to turn around, and after 5 years it reached the highest level ever. I looked at the chart of the mutual fund where my money was invested, and I thought, "Great! I have been investing in this fund when the prices were very low and now they are very high. I made a lot of money!"

Now, you won't believe what happened next. I went to the insurance company to terminate the policy because, at that time, I started to realize what a fraud this can all be. I realized that they probably took a lot of my gains through fees and commissions but nothing prepared me for what happened next...

During the 5 years, I paid exactly $12,005 in premiums and more than 95% of that money was supposed to go towards the investment part of the policy. So, I did a quick calculation that showed that I should get at least 45% return on my investment. That is, the cash value of my policy should be around $16,530. Buying low and selling high is always a good thing, isn't it?

So, I'm sitting in the office with the insurance company's employee, who was in charge of policy termination. The office is a typical financial institution office. She is a very nice, official-looking lady with glasses. After a couple of minutes of typing, she printed out the final policy statement and gave it to me.

When I saw the number, I just stared in disbelief.

The cash value of my policy was $9,277. And then there was another fee that the financial advisor didn't tell me about – $2,261 in insurance costs. I was shocked.

What I got out of this "safe" investment was a cash value of $7,016. $4,989 less than I paid in premiums.

Despite the fact that I made all my investments when the price of the mutual fund was low and the fund was at the highest point in history when I sold, my return was a staggering minus 42%!

I don't want to even think about people who buy similar policies and hope to finance their pensions with them, or who buy them in times when the market conditions are less favorable than in my example.

These things shouldn't happen to people who are working hard to earn their money, only to lose it because of the greed of the financial industry. In my opinion, it's simply not ethical to sell these kinds of products, but the financial industry does it all the time.

## "Knowing the right detail gets you a great return. Ignore them and you just crash & burn."

**@RobertRolih #MillionDollarDecision**

What was my real cost of this policy? To understand how much I really lost, you also need to take into account the opportunity costs. That means that we need to ask ourselves how much more I would have made if I invested in an alternative investment that had less commissions and fees. If I took 95% of my premiums and I invested them in one of the low-cost financial products I talk about in the next chapter, I would get at least a 45% return in the same period, and that is a conservative estimate.

So, the amount of money I would have made if I just chose a better financial vehicle would be at least $16,530. That means I lost $9,514, and that is a conservative estimate.

How is this possible? Because all the combined insurance/investment products have very high commissions and fees. It was the fees and commissions that cost me $9,514.

That is why you should never combine investments and insurance!

What about the life insurance products or other annuity products that promise 100% of the market returns on up years and no loss on down years?

These products are a dime a dozen and they look fantastic. Who wouldn't want to have only the upside with no downside?

One of my clients showed me the brochure for one of these products. It was given to him by his financial planner just days before he attended my seminar.

When I went through the brochure, I said to myself, "That's too good to be true! If this product is really that good, I want it now!"

So, I did a little research, and what I found out is that these products are really too good to be true. The harsh reality is that the brochures are promising a lot, but if you dig deeper into the small print, and you do an in-depth analysis, you find out that the best outcome over the long run is that you end up with less than one-third of market returns - a far cry from the promised 100% on the up years and no downside.

## "When something seems too good to be true, it usually is."

### @RobertRolih #MillionDollarDecision

People are being misled all the time because you need to be almost a mathematical genius to understand how these products work in reality. It's simply appalling that these kinds of products are even legal, and worse yet, financial advisers and insurance agents are offering them to their clients very aggressively. Why? Because they earn a lot of money by doing so, and most of the time they don't even understand the products themselves.

That was the third part of the A.R.M.O.R. formula™. Never combine investments and insurance!

## Three Secret Strategies to Lower the Cost of Your Insurance

**A.R.M.o.R. FoRMULA™**

ASSESS THE RISK FACTORS
REVIEW INSURANCE COMPANIES
MAKE INVESTMENTS SEPARATELY
O
R

When buying insurance, most people think that the prices or premiums that the insurance companies charge are set in stone. After all, you are dealing with a big company. No way will they be willing to negotiate the premiums. Right? Wrong!

For some insurance policies that you buy, you may be able to negotiate a quote to get a lower price. The first rule of negotiating is: always ask for a discount. It costs you nothing to ask! The worst thing that can happen is that they say, "No."

So how to negotiate the best possible deal and optimize your costs?

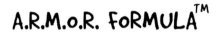

# A.R.M.o.R. FoRMULA™

**A**SSESS THE RISK FACToRS
**R**EVIEW INSURANCE CoMPANIES
**M**AKE INVESTMENTS SEPARATELY
**O**PTIMIZE THE CoSTS
**R**

Let me help you with my three best negotiating tactics. These tactics work the best when you are in a personal meeting or on the phone with your broker. These also work for almost any important buying situation.

## 1. God Guy, Bad Guy

You have seen this technique many times in crime movies. A crime suspect is caught and interrogated in an interrogation room. The first, scary looking detective puts him under a glaring light, hits him with hard questions, threatens him and roughs him up. Then he leaves and in comes the nice detective who gives the suspect a cup of coffee and lets him relax. After some sweet talk and assurances that he will get away with a light sentence, the suspect spills all he knows.

This is a classic example of a "god guy, bad guy" negotiating technique. And you can use it too.

Ask your spouse to be with you when you talk with your insurance broker and agree on a role with him or her. The bad guy will complain about the price, whine about how hard it is to afford all these insurance policies, and that he/she prefers other insurance companies.

And the good guy will side with the broker, tell him nicely that he should make a better offer to try and calm things down.

# If you want a better price, you better ask for it.

### @RobertRolih #MillionDollarDecision

Many times just the pressure from this technique can bring the price quote down.

## 2. Anchoring

Let's say, for example, that you are in the process of buying a new suit.

In the first scenario, you go into a store and a nice shopping attendant first shows you a $2,000 suit. After a while, she shows you an $800 suit.

In the second scenario, she first shows you a $500 suit, and then an $800 one.

Studies show that you would be much more likely to buy a suit in the first scenario. Why? Because your psychological anchor was set to $2,000 first. And any price that is lower than that will seem less expensive. In short, your perception of the same suit would be influenced by the price of the first suit you saw.

Anchoring negotiation strategy refers to the human tendency to heavily rely on the first piece of information offered when making decisions.

So, how do you use this technique when buying insurance? There are two ways.

First, get some online price quotes for the insurance policy. Then, call your broker and tell him that you are looking for an XYZ insurance policy, and add, "I already got some quotes from different insurance companies, but I'm not satisfied with the price." You can bet that he will ask you what kinds of quotes you already got. Here is where you can use some anchors – tell him the lowest quotes.

By doing that, he will be psychologically influenced to give you better quotes.

The second way to use that is when you already have a quote from your broker. You can call him or her and say something like this: "I got your quote, but boy, it's much more expensive than the others I got from XYZ and W insurance company. They are offering to sell me the same insurance policy for $X less."

Again, your broker will be psychologically influenced to give you a better quote.

## 3. Combining

This one is very straightforward. Insurance companies will give you a better deal if you buy more than one insurance policy from them. When they see that you can give them more business, they will make you a better deal.

So just ask your broker questions like these:

- How much would I save if I buy car insurance and term life insurance with you?
- How much would I save if I also transfer my house insurance to your company?

Just by buying multiple policies from one company, can get you a discount. So it pays to ask.

# *Details That Can Ruin Your Life*

Recently, I read an article about a man who traveled to Australia to attend his daughter's wedding. He bought a travel insurance policy from a big insurance company, as almost all travelers should.

The day before his daughter's wedding, he slipped on some steps and suffered serious head and brain injuries. Unfortunately, he had drunk a couple of bottles of beer before that and when trying to claim his insurance benefit, his insurance company pointed to a standard exclusion clause.

That clause, buried in the small print, invalidates claims when alcohol is a factor. They refused to pay his hospital bills, and, as you can imagine these bills were huge.

All insurance policies are contracts; that is why many of the important items are often found in the small print. Small print is the part of the contract where all the exclusions are stated.

The exclusions are very important, because many people buy an insurance policy, think that they are covered for certain risks and find out that they aren't - only when it's too late.

For example, before I signed my life insurance policy, I checked the small print and found out that if I die as a result of a terrorist attack, my family gets nothing. I called my broker and I negotiated to change this clause with no extra costs.

When I got a new version of the contract, the small print said that my family gets a benefit if I die in a terrorist attack, as long as I'm not the terrorist, and since I will never be one, I signed the contract.

Again: read the small print very carefully, and if something is not to your liking, talk to your agent or insurance company and ask them to change it. The competition is very strong in the insurance industry, so most insurance companies will negotiate with you regarding these exclusions.

## A.R.M.O.R. FORMULA™

ASSESS THE RISK FACTORS
REVIEW INSURANCE COMPANIES
MAKE INVESTMENTS SEPARATELY
OPTIMIZE THE COSTS
READ THE SMALL PRINT

The main clauses you should pay attention to in the small print are:

# Contestability period

When you sign your insurance policy, be very careful, because most of them have a so-called "contestability period." This means that during a certain period of time, usually two years from issue, the insurance company has the right to cancel the coverage or deny a claim if they find that an omission was made at the time of the application.

For example, if you didn't mention that you have a heart condition in your application, the insurance company has the right to cancel your policy if they find that out during the contestability period. Even if you, for example, died from a completely different cause, the insurance company can refuse to pay your beneficiaries if your death occurred during the contestability period and they can prove you didn't disclose your heart condition. So, don't withhold any information to get lower rates.

# Material misrepresentation clause

This clause means that if a person intentionally withholds information from the insurer that would have resulted in them not insuring him or her, the insurance company has the right to cancel the policy. This clause is permanent, unlike the contestability period, which is only effective for a period of time.

# Suicide clause

Almost all life insurance policies have a suicide clause. Under this clause, the life insurance company will not pay the death benefit if the insured commits suicide within the first two years of the policy. The only payment the insurance company will make is the return of premiums paid. After two years, the policy will pay out, even if the cause of death is suicide. This protects the insurance company from people purchasing insurance with the intention of committing suicide to provide their beneficiaries with a death benefit.

### Illegal or dangerous activity

Insurance companies could deny a claim for a death benefit in the case of life insurance if you die while conducting an illegal or dangerous activity. For example, if you like car racing, and you die during a race, your claim could be denied. For dangerous activities, it is often possible to negotiate inclusion in their policy for a small extra cost. As for illegal activities, I'm not so sure.

## *The Amazing Insurance Policy that Costs You Nothing*

There are two levels of protection you can employ, if you want to sleep well at night and if you want to provide you and your family financial protection and safety.

The first level is something you can **buy**. These were the insurance policies we just talked about.

The second level is something you can **do**.

The second level of protection costs you nothing, but it can be the best insurance policy imaginable.

Let's face it. Your quality of life is largely dependent on your physical health. If you are also financially well off, then you can really live the life of your dreams, but, without physical well-being, your quality of life drops significantly.

## "Health is just like money. We never grasp the value of it until we lose it."

@RobertRolih #MillionDollarDecision

So, the second insurance policy you should take care of is maintaining a healthy lifestyle. Now, I don't mean that you should work out two hours per day, eat only healthy food and go into all kinds of extremes. I believe that you can have a very healthy lifestyle without a big effort.

I'm far from being an expert on health, fitness and food, but most research shows that you can maintain a healthy lifestyle if you just follow these simple steps:

- **Exercise regularly.** A 30-minute walk every day does the trick – no need to use all the equipment they try to sell you on TV. It also helps to have sex often.

- **Eat less sugar.** One of the best things you can do to improve your health is to eliminate soft drinks and eat less (or no) sugary food.

- **Drink more water.** Water purifies your body, and many health problems are linked to your body not having enough water and other fluids to carry out its normal functions.

- **Eat less meat and more vegetables.** Hundreds of studies show that eating less meat improves your health, increases the level of energy you have and reduces your risk of heart disease and other chronic conditions.

That's it. Four simple things anybody can do.

Although there are thousands of different diets and philosophies about health out there, pretty much all of them are based on these four things. So, if you just follow these simple steps, you will be far healthier than most people.

Like I said, I'm no expert on this topic, so you should check some books and online resources to learn more about it. Just be careful when you see a health "guru" who gives advice in order to sell his line of food supplements. Food supplements are, in most cases, totally ineffective or even harmful[16]. Unfortunately, these products have a high-profit margin, which makes them very lucrative to sell. For more information about that, I recommend you to read the book *Bad Science* by Ben Goldacre.

To summarize, when you lead a healthy lifestyle, you decrease the probability (although you can never decrease it to zero) of cancer, heart disease and other major health problems. Plus, your ability to make more money will increase as your energy level does.

## *All That is Gold Does Not Glitter*

Now you protected yourself in case something happens to you, but what if something really bad happens to the whole world we live in?

If there is an alien invasion or if the planet blows up, there is nothing you can do, but what about wars, hyperinflation or natural disasters? These and similar things are certainly a possibility.

That is why it's good to have some extra protection on hand in case any of them happens. I'm not talking about guns, even though in the case of war they would come in handy. I'm talking about gold.

Gold has a special role in human history. It was associated with gods and kings. Wars were fought over it. It was used as money and store of value. If you had gold, you had power and you had glory. In recent history, whole continents were transformed because of the gold rushes in the 19th century.

Many people ask me what is so special about gold for it to be so valuable, and such a popular investment. Let me explain it with a short science fiction story that will show you the answer.

A long time ago in a galaxy far, far away, there was a strange life-form that vaguely resembled a panda. Strangely enough, they called themselves Pandas. They were happy creatures that had a very different body chemistry compared to humans. Their main food was gold. They just couldn't survive without it, but as luck has it, their planet was full of gold. Everywhere you would look on their yellow planet, you would see gold.

For millions of years, they lived happily on their planet, eating gold, taking care of their babies, writing poetry and attending yoga classes. Then a Panda prodigy with a name that we couldn't pronounce discovered something frightening. After years of study, he concluded that because of the population growth, the planet's supplies of gold would last for only another 100 years.

The Pandas needed to act quickly. They banned yoga classes and poetry and focused all of their energy to build giant antennas to locate other planets that could be their future sources of food.

After years of listening to the sky, they found an alien signal. It was a radio transmission from a distant planet. When they translated the radio transmission, they found out that it was a radio interview with Robert Kiyosaki. Pandas certainly didn't care about Kiyosaki, but they cared very much for the part in the interview where Kiyosaki told the audience that the dollar has a very bleak future, and that we should all buy gold.

Now that really got the attention of Pandas. If you could understand what they were yelling in ecstasy, it would translate to something like, "Yes! Gold! Gold! Kiyosaki is our savior!"

So, Pandas started to build a giant spaceship the size of the moon that would transport all the gold they could find on the distant planet, back home. They equipped the spaceship with a huge, cutting edge magnet that only attracted gold.

You see, Pandas were very harmless creatures and they didn't want to annihilate the poor alien beings. They even invented something called the Prime Directive that would prohibit starship personnel from interfering with the internal development of alien civilizations. They even deployed some independent United Panda officials to oversee that.

On the day that the spaceship arrived at its target planet, there was a big, planet-wide party, organized on the planet of Pandas. All the Pandas were ready to celebrate their hero spaceship crew, and, through the marvel of science, they could even watch the whole story unfolding live on their intergalactic hyper-space TV.

If you would sit in front of one of those TV's, you would see that there is this enormous spaceship approaching a strange blue-white planet. For the first time, the blue planet seemed to have two moons of almost equal size. Then the spaceship stops.

The gold magnet starts to unfold.

It's really a magnificent sight. All the Pandas around you are silently staring at their TV screens. Then, the crew activates the magnet. In a minute all the gold from the blue planet should be attracted to the magnet and then stored in the spaceship. If there will be more gold than anticipated, they would of course repeat the trip.

"And there it is!" goes the TV reporter, "Success! The first small pile of gold is approaching the spaceship!" You can see that it's the size of a three-story house.

All the Pandas on the home planet start to cheer. "Ok, the main mass of the gold, our salvation, should fly over in a second!" continues the reporter.

But nothing happens.

A couple of minutes go by.

Nothing.

The crew checks the magnet, checks all the other systems and there is no malfunction.

Then the captain announces, "All systems are working fine. That's all there is…"

And then…all the hell breaks loose on the Panda planet.

TV stations start to broadcast the aftermath. Peaceful pandas are rioting and shooting each other. They break into convenience stores and grab what is left of the gold. The last scene the Pandas see before the TV signal goes out is a panda preacher with a sign saying, "The end is near."

How did I do? Do you think that this story could be made into a blockbuster movie? If so, please write an email to Steven Spielberg. I appreciate your support! LOL!

Gold, gold, gold. The key to understanding gold is to understand just how little of it we have mined in our history.

# "Gold is special. It always was and probably always will be, at least till the ancient dream of alchemy – turning lead into gold – becomes more than just a dream."

### @RobertRolih #MillionDollarDecision

There are many different sources of data about gold, and their estimates of how much gold has been mined in history range from 160,000 to 200,000 metric tons[17]. This quantity is very hard to imagine, so let me give you a better perspective. All the gold in the world would fit into 3 to 4 Olympic pools, or in a very big villa. That's it. That's all the gold in the world. That is why the Pandas faced death from hunger even though they took all of our gold.

In the last 2,500 years, gold (and often also silver) has been used throughout the world as money or a trading medium. Before the introduction of paper money, people traded by using gold coins. The first gold coins appeared in Asia Minor around 600 B.C., and people loved it because of its density (gold is very heavy) and ease by which it could be melted.

And even once paper money was introduced all over the world, most currencies maintained an explicit link to gold. That meant that the paper money could be exchanged for gold on demand and that you could only print a limited quantity of money. All the paper money needed to have a gold backing.

By the late 19th Century, many of the world's major currencies were fixed to gold. That was called a Gold Standard. But then World War I broke out, and many countries decided to suspend or abandon the Gold Standard. That meant that the central banks could print money at will, and some of them did just that.

The most famous example of this was the German central bank that, in the aftermath of World War I, issued enormous sums of paper money to support workers who were on strike against the French occupation, and to pay for war reparations. This led to the German hyperinflation of the early 1920s, between June 1921 and January 1924[18]. In the first half of 1921, the mark exchange rate vs. U.S. dollar was 90, and by November 1923, you needed 4,210,500,000,000 German marks to buy one U.S. dollar. Just imagine how they transported this amount of paper money.

After World War II, the Gold Standard was successfully reestablished under the Bretton Woods system. It did well for 3 decades, but was abandoned again in 1971 when the U.S. government refused to redeem its dollars in gold.

Today, fiat or paper money is used for most monetary roles all around the world. Fiat money is currency that is legal tender in a country, but is not backed by a physical commodity. Fiat money is based solely on faith. As long as we trust our government, the money has value for us. That value derives from the relationship between supply and demand. If our governments print more money, the money loses its value. We can all see that in the price increases of all the products and services we buy, and we call it inflation.

What does this mean for us?

It means that, as long as our economic system works, everything is fine. But if something terrible happens in the world, we are in trouble.

That is why my relationship with gold is very simple.

I don't use gold as an investment, but as insurance. I have some gold just in case something really bad happens in this world, and I hope that I will die with that gold still intact. I don't use gold as an investment but as an insurance policy in case one of these scenarios happen:

## Scenario 1: The collapse of currencies

We know that central banks increase the money supply all the time. That leads to inflation – a slow rise of prices. Hyperinflation happens when the printing of money gets out of control. Because of the uncertainty in the future worth of currency, people panic and start buying physical things, or whatever of value they can find, as fast as they can. This causes the paper money to be worth less and less because there is just too much of it on the market and everybody tries to get rid of it.

There are many books, financial gurus, and other prophets who warn us of the "Coming Collapse," or "The Dollar Crisis," or "The End of Our Economic System." They try to convince you to invest heavily in gold because the world's currencies, and maybe even the whole world order, will collapse. I also know that their main motivation in saying that is because they want to sell their services, books and courses.

Bad news and prophecies about gold price are always in demand. So, if you want to earn some easy money, start preaching about the end of our economic system and sell gold to panic-stricken people. Now, if you want to really make a lot of money, set up your own religion, indoctrinate your believers, sell them fake gold and then make a run for it. This has been done again and again, and it will work in the future, because, like Albert Einstein once said, "Only two things are infinite: the universe and human stupidity, and I'm not sure about the former."

Now seriously: is there a possibility that the collapse of currencies and even a total collapse of our civilization will happen? Yes. I think it's a small one, but still – the possibility exists. Now, what can happen if this scenario comes to life?

Just think of apocalypse movies like Mad Max, or the TV series like The Walking Dead (with more people alive, I hope) and you will get the picture. In the resulting chaos, people would go back to bartering. If you survived, you would need food, guns, fuel and shelter. So, if you have a cow and you needed a gun, you could trade a cow for two guns. I just made the number up because I'm not sure what the exchange rate of cows to guns would be.

After a while, people would start to form small societies, and there would be a growing need for a trade medium or money. But let's face it - you don't always want to exchange a cow for a gun. Maybe you need some clothes, and in that case, precious metals will probably start to perform the function of money as they have for thousands of years.

## Scenario 2: The next World War

I think there is a very small possibility of a widespread, all-out war in the foreseeable future. The world is now more interconnected and interdependent on each other. If we just take a look at the global trade interdependency, you can quickly see that the supply chains for any complex product are zigzagging all over the world. So, in the case of a world war, global trade comes to a standstill and nobody wins.

Maybe the most important argument that puts the possibility of this scenario to a really small number is the fact of mutually assured destruction. After World War II, we lived in a world where atomic weapons could simply destroy our planet, if used in an all-out war. If one big power used them, so would the others. In that case, neither money nor gold could help any of us. Your only hope would be to build a nuclear shelter somewhere near your house.

Even though an all-out war is not likely, it's still a possibility. There is always some crazy egomaniacal leader in the world that can do something crazy and start a war. So, let's say that a big conflict happens and that the nuclear weapons are not being used. In that case, currencies could still perform their role, but if they break down, keep in mind that gold retains its value during wars and major crises. Gold is the only respected currency when paper money loses its value.

## Scenario 3: The invasion of bloodthirsty alien Pandas

Now this one is a real danger. If the Pandas are in a really bloodthirsty mood, and they land on our planet, gold could save your life. So, if a Panda stands in front of you with a laser rifle, you could try to buy your way out of certain death by bribing it with some gold.

Ok, as we see, all these scenarios are unlikely, but certainly possible. That is why it is a smart move to have some gold (and possibly silver), but just don't overdo it. Investing 50% of your investable money in gold and silver would be overkill. In my opinion, investing 5% to 15% of your investable money is more than enough to have basic insurance in case something bad happens.

## *The Big Mistakes When Buying Gold*

Ok, now you know that you need to buy some gold (and silver) - where do you get it? And how do you avoid the costly mistakes people make when buying it? To give you the most up-to-date guidelines, I prepared a special *Precious Metals* section on The Million Dollar Decision members-only website. To get access, visit www.MillionDollarDecisionBook.com/bonus now.

Let me summarize: gold is a great tool that you need to use to insure yourself and your family in case anything terrible happens in our world. It's a safety tool and not an investing tool. That is why I recommend having some gold in the physical form stored somewhere safe near where you live. But if you own gold as an investment where you expect good returns, there is a high probability that you will be disappointed.

Having the right insurance policies, living a healthy lifestyle, plus owning some physical gold, is a good formula for financial security. After you take care of these things, it's time to get some good investing returns. I will show you how to do it in the next chapter. As you will see, the way to do it is quite counterintuitive.

## *The Million Dollar Action Plan*

- A list of the key questions to ask your insurance agent when you are buying different types of insurance policies. Download it here: www.MillionDollarDecisionBook.com/bonus

- Avoid the costly mistakes when buying gold and silver! Get step-by-step instructions on how and where to buy them. I constantly keep this resource up to date, and it will save you a lot of time and help you avoid the biggest mistakes people make when buying precious metals. Get it here: www.MillionDollarDecisionBook.com/bonus

*"Whenever you find yourself on the side of the majority, it is time to pause and reflect."*

– Mark Twain

# Chapter 5

---

## Gone with the Wind: Where Do Your Long-Term Investing Returns End Up?

---

**Y**ou can't win the financial game by playing only defensively.

Now that you have taken care of your basic financial safety with insurance products and gold, it's time to make your money work for you and get some good returns. There are several ways to do this, but the one that should get the most of your attention is long-term investing.

My best definition of long-term investing is simply buying a financial instrument; for example, a stock, bond or fund, and holding it for at least 10 years. This is in sharp contrast to short-term investing or speculating, where your holding period is usually measured in days or months.

There are a lot of good reasons why we invest for the long run. Let me name just a few:

- Growing your retirement pot, which helps you build peace of mind for the future.

- Providing your family with a safety cushion of assets that further increases your financial safety and financial power.

- Building assets that grow and provide you with passive income streams.

- Investing returns that are almost impossible to beat with any other investing strategy.

Because of these reasons, long-term investing is something almost anybody should be doing. But there is a problem with long-term investing. A big problem.

The problem we face is that the financial industry is aggressively selling long-term investing products that are the most profitable for them and not for the investors. These are the products that have the highest commissions and fees. Even though these fees seem low at first sight, they can wreak chaos in your financial life.

Most people, even experienced investors, are not even aware of the effect of commissions on their long-term investments.

In this chapter, I will lead you through the maze of long-term investing, where most people fall prey to the claws of the financial industry. I will help you finally cut through that maze, and find a very simple solution that will enable you to outperform 19 out of 20 investors, with a time commitment of only a couple hours per year!

Sounds good?

OK, let me lead the way!

# The One Investing Concept to Rule Them All

If you haven't lived on the dark side of the moon for the last decade, you have probably heard of the movie trilogy, *The Lord of the Rings*.

The main plot of the series revolves around a magic ring that has an extraordinary amount of power. It's called the One Ring. Its creator forged it to gain control over the remaining 19 rings of power that were worn by the rulers of the different races appearing in the movie. The other, lesser rings, were linked to the power of the One Ring, and were dependent on it. So, whoever wore the One Ring, could control all the other leaders wearing lesser rings.

Why am I telling you that? Because, in the world of investing, there is also a concept that rules all other investing concepts (sorry, I know that a magical investing ring would be more fun.)

If you understand this concept, you will understand long-term investing, and, ultimately, wealth building, and you will have the power to win the financial game of life.

If you don't, then nothing will make sense, and the financial industry will always be able to take advantage of you.

Because this concept can be somewhat puzzling to understand, I will introduce it to you with the help of a fictional story. So let's have some fun while learning about it!

My neighbor is an amateur magician whose stage name is Gandalf. A couple of months ago, my wife and I went on a vacation, and I asked him if he could feed our tropical fish while we were away. He said, "Sure, no problem. As long as you feed my magical rabbits for one month when I go on a vacation this summer," and he pointed to two nice white rabbits that were playing in the corner. "They are clean and nice, and your children will love them! They just have this one procreation problem. Because they are magical rabbits, they tend to double in numbers every night while I'm not around." "It's a deal!" I replied with a smile, thinking that he was joking. Oh boy, if I only knew what awaited me!

Then, summer came and one day Gandalf comes by with his rabbits: "Here you go! I'm leaving today, and here are my rabbits."

My three year old and five year old kids jumped in excitement, took the rabbits and hugged them. And I thought: "Looks like they will have a good time for the next month."

The next day I woke up, and I quickly found out that there were four rabbits jumping around the living room. "Hmmm… I must have overlooked two of them yesterday…"

Next day. Surprise, surprise! There were eight rabbits when I entered the living room.

And then I remembered what Gandalf said about the procreation issue. "Ok, not a big problem. They seem to be doubling every day. But it's only for one month. We will take care of a few rabbits," I told my wife.

If you went by my house the day after that, you would hear me screaming, "What have you done, Gandalf! My house is turning into an animal farm!" because there were already 16 of them.

After ten days, there were more than a thousand rabbits running around. If you think that having two rabbits at home is not easy, think about all the food that I needed now to feed this army of rabbits!

After 20 days, if you could count them all, you would count 1,048,576 of them! Now, this number is a bit hard to illustrate and my designer gave up at this point.

Finally, on the 30th day, Gandalf came home, but at that time, the whole country was swamped with more than 1 billion rabbits! They even formed a rabbit government that demanded that rabbits should have equal rights to humans.

And, if Gandalf didn't intervene then, there would be 8.5 billion rabbits by day 33, and rabbits would rule the world! This would be the official death of the human race!

**Exhibit 5.1** Rabbit population growth

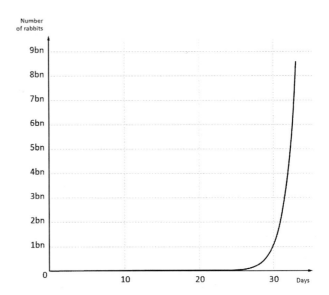

| Days | Number of rabbits |
|------|-------------------|
| 1 | 2 |
| 2 | 4 |
| 3 | 8 |
| 4 | 16 |
| 5 | 32 |
| 6 | 64 |
| 7 | 128 |
| 8 | 256 |
| 9 | 512 |
| 10 | 1,024 |
| ... | |
| 20 | 1,048,576 |
| ... | |
| 30 | 1,073,741,824 |
| ... | |
| 33 | 8,589,934,592 |

So…what happened there? How on Earth could I tell my wife, on the third day, that we would have no problem managing a few magical rabbits for 30 days?

The answer is that I underestimated the effect of one of the most important mathematical concepts. It's called "compounding," or "compound interest," and you just saw its amazing power that nearly destroyed the human race.

This concept is quite magical when you stop to think about it. It greatly affects all long-term investments and it can work wonders with your invested money.

The technical definition of compound interest, which you can find on Investopedia, goes like this: "Compound interest is interest added to the principal of a deposit or loan, so that the added interest also earns interest from then on. This addition of interest to the principal is called compounding."

In the rabbit story I just told you, rabbits doubled in number every day. In technical terms, that would mean a 100% daily interest rate. Of course, in the world of investing, you can only dream about this kind of return.

So, what is a realistic return that you can get when you are investing for the long run? Well, it depends. But for the next segment of the book, I will use 10% annual interest, or growth. 10% was the average annual historical return for stocks, which, like I said before, may or may not continue in the future.

**Exhibit 5.2** $1,000 invested for 40 years at 10%, compounded annually

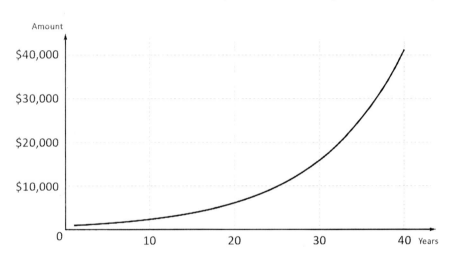

As you can see, the growth is slow in the beginning, but later on it becomes exponential, as the differences between time periods grow larger and larger. In short, compounding works best over longer time periods. The longer the time period, the more money you accumulate. That is why a small investment of $1,000 grows to $41,145 in 40 years, and that is also the reason why my definition of long-term investing says that you need to hold the financial instrument for at least 10 years.

In real life, we don't usually invest a lump sum of money once in a lifetime, but we invest a part of the money we make every year, or even every month. So what happens if you not only invest $1,000 one time, but you make annual additions of $1,000?

Let's take a look:

**Exhibit 5.3** Investing $1,000 a year at 10%, compounded annually

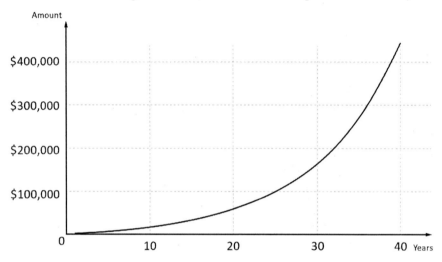

Now, that's powerful. An annual investment of just $1,000 builds a substantial amount of money over a long period of time. That is why Albert Einstein said that compound interest is "the most powerful force in the universe."

Albert Einstein was a very smart man; so smart that he produced the world's most famous equation: $E = mc^2$. He also developed the general theory of relativity, another very talked about subject, even though most people don't understand one iota of it (myself included). And if he said that compound interest is the most powerful force in the universe, we better take advantage of it.

To summarize, compounding is the most powerful concept in long-term investing. It's like the One Ring that rules all the other rings in *The Lord of the Rings,* and in the next chapters, I will show you how you can use it to fast forward your wealth.

## *Let's Talk Products*

Do you agree that long-term investing is a good idea? If not, now's a good time to put this book away.

If yes, then you are probably asking yourself what to invest in.

Here is where most people make a big mistake – they invest in the wrong financial products – the ones that are destroying their financial future. The ones where the financial industry makes a lot of money and investors remain empty handed. It's not their fault. That decision is usually heavily influenced by the advice they get on TV, from popular investing websites, from their financial adviser, broker or banker.

Like I mentioned earlier, these people are rewarded handsomely when they sell you financial products that work for them and not for you.

## "The most popular investing products are the worst ones for investors."

### @RobertRolih #MillionDollarDecision

That is why making the right decision – a Million Dollar Decision – is the essence of this book.

I lost a lot of money in my investing career because I made incorrect decisions when I started investing. The decision to trust my financial advisers, money managers and some financial "gurus" also caused me stress and many sleepless nights. I wrote this chapter so you don't have to go through the same financial hell that I did.

But let's go step by step. First, let's determine what are the best options for long-term investing; ones that will allow you to significantly grow your money.

If we take another look at the Financial Success Formula™, we can see that financial success is the result of your Money Making activities, where you need to be very aggressive, and the investing activities where you need to be very careful and where you employ strategies that don't take a lot of time. In other words, you employ passive strategies where money works for you - without you lifting a finger.

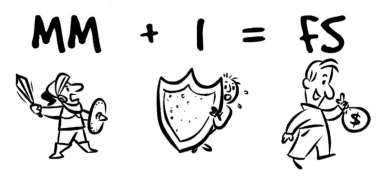

So what are the options for long-term investing that fit these criteria?

Let's take a look at them:

A. Stocks

B. Bonds

C. Precious metals

D. Bank deposits

E. Or, you can just keep your money under the mattress

A good question at this point would be where to invest your money; an even better question could be where NOT to invest your money. That is why we will first eliminate some really bad options.

The silliest option to eliminate right away is, of course, keeping your money under the mattress. The reason why is that money doesn't grow under the mattress, and, even worse, inflation makes it lose value over time. Inflation is an important factor we need to take into account when we are investing. In simple terms, inflation means that your money is worth less and less over time, because of the general increase in prices.

Let me give you an everyday example. The average price for a pound of white bread was $0.70 in 1990. Today, it's three times that, and the same goes for almost all products[19]. That is why keeping money under the mattress is not a smart move - if mice don't eat it, inflation will eat it up over time.

What about bank deposits? Certainly, they are a better option compared to the previous one, but not by much. Bank savings account interest rates are so low that they don't even cover inflation. So, if you save your money in the bank, you are losing money when you account for inflation.

Next, precious metals. We already talked about gold in the previous chapter. There, we established that gold tends to maintain its value over time. That means that, when we account for the inflation, there is no real return when you own it. That is why I use gold as protection and not as an investment that would give me good returns.

So, we are left with the first two options: stocks and bonds. And these two options are, in my opinion, the only two options suitable for passive long-term investing.

Historically, stocks were, by far, the better option compared to bonds. They are the only option that builds your wealth quickly, as historically they've had approximately 10% average annual returns. Will it be the same in the future? We don't know for sure, but I think that, because of the nature of stocks, they will almost certainly outperform all other asset classes in the future. Why? Because when you invest in stocks, you are investing in companies that are bringing new value to the market, are constantly innovating, growing and adapting to the new market realities.

# "Stocks were historically by far, the best option for long-term investing and it's highly probable that they will stay the best in the future."

**@RobertRolih #MillionDollarDecision**

So let's pick some stocks!

Let's pick Apple, Coca-Cola, Nike, Amazon and some others.

Is this a good idea?

The answer is, of course, "No."

Investing in a small number of stocks is very risky, and you don't want to bet your financial future on that. Why?

**The first reason** is that any company can go down, or even out of business. There is a high probability that, over the course of a couple of decades, many of the companies that are household names now will go out of business, or will just become average. How do we know that? Because it has happened, again and again, throughout history.

If you compare the list of Fortune 500 companies 10 years ago and today, you can see that almost half of the companies on the list are no longer there today[20]. If you go back in time to the year 1955, and you make the same comparison, you will find out that there are only 61 names on both lists. In other words, almost 9 out of 10 companies from 1955 have either gone bankrupt, merged or are mediocre companies today.

This is a sign of constant technological advances, innovation and healthy competition.

So for example, if you pick 5 stocks and bet your financial future and retirement on them, you are very likely to end up with a couple of losing stocks. If 2 companies out of 5 go out of business (a very likely scenario over a couple of decades), the remaining 3 stocks would need to go up by 67% in order for you to just break even.

# "Any company in the world can go out of business."

### @RobertRolih #MillionDollarDecision

**The second reason** why you don't want to invest in individual stocks is that, even if you think that you can pick the right stocks – the ones that will outperform the market – your chances of being successful are very, very small.

Alfred Cowles III was the first to study the accuracy of financial analyst forecasts. In 1933, he published an article titled, "Can Stock Market Forecasters Forecast?"[21] His study was thoroughly researched and mathematically sound, and in it he examined the recommendations of 36 investment firms that provided research on individual stocks between 1928 and 1932. On average, their recommendations underperformed the average market returns by 1.3% a year.

But these were different times, you might ask. Surely now, with all the computing power and easier access to information, stock pickers would be more successful.

The answer is, "No."

Study after study shows that professionals who pick the stocks have no edge over average market returns. One of the most comprehensive studies that proved this was done by professors Laurent Barras, Olivier Scaillet and Russell Wermers, who analyzed the performance of 2,076 professionals over a 32-year time period from 1975 to 2006.

Their conclusion? 99.4% of these managers displayed no evidence of genuine stock picking skill, and the 0.6% of managers who did outperform the market, were "statistically indistinguishable from zero."

If the professionals can't do it, maybe individual, amateur investors can!

Again, the answer is "No." Brad M. Barber and Terrance Odean, from the University of California, studied and analyzed the trading records of 10,000 brokerage accounts of individual investors over a seven-year period[23]. They wanted to see how good individual investors were at picking stocks.

They identified all instances in which an investor sold one stock and soon afterward bought another stock. Their thinking was that the investor thought that the stock he bought would do better than the one he sold.

Then, they analyzed the returns of both stocks over the following year. On average, the stock the investors sold did far better than those they bought. The difference was a whopping 3.3 percentage points, and that didn't even account for the effect of commissions and fees.

# "Trying to pick the stocks that outperform the average is like trying to find a needle in a haystack."

**@RobertRolih #MillionDollarDecision**

To summarize: we all think that we are smart, above average and that we have amazing predictive powers. Professionals even make a living out of convincing others that this is true, but the harsh reality is that we are all losers from the start if we try to pick individual stocks.

So what to do now? We established that stocks were historically the best option for long-term investing, but picking stocks is too risky, and can be outright dangerous for your financial future. Here is where the financial industry got a great idea.

# *Financial Industry to the Rescue! Really?*

Because of the very risky nature of investing in individual stocks, the financial industry proposed a solution. The fact is that you can never reliably predict the price movement of an individual stock, but, in the long run, you can very reliably predict the movement of the entire stock market. The stock market has a very powerful trend of growth over the long run, and there are no signs that this trend will stop anytime soon.

Yes, there are a lot of sharp, short-term ups and downs in the stock market, but in the long run, they don't really matter. After every crisis, there was also a period of rising prices and, always, new all-time highs after the crisis. For example, after the financial crisis of 2009, stocks needed just four years to pick up and make a new all-time high.

Now, you are probably asking yourself if this trend will continue. The answer is that anything is possible, but I think that the probability of that trend changing is very low. Stocks will very likely continue to grow over the long run, because companies constantly innovate, bring new value to the market and adapt to the new market conditions.

So what was the financial industry's solution? It was quite simple and effective: "Why don't we put 100, 500 or a 1,000 stocks in one basket or one product, and sell this product to investors?"

And the product called *mutual fund* was born. So, when you buy a mutual fund, you buy many stocks – a basket of stocks – at the same time.

Now, let me ask you a question. Do mutual funds solve the problem of the risk of investing in a small selection of individual stocks?

The answer is "Yes." If you buy hundreds of stocks, you lower that risk, and that makes the mutual fund a very attractive investing vehicle. That is why more than 50 million U.S. households own mutual funds.

So why don't I recommend that you invest in mutual funds, even though they are the most popular, long-term investing choice all around the world?

The answer is because of the commissions and fees.

# The Devil In Disguise

In my opinion, there are two main reasons why mutual funds are the most popular long-term investing vehicles.

The first is that the basic product benefit of a mutual fund is a very sound one. Compared to stock picking, owning a lot of stocks is a much better and safer solution for long-term investors.

The second reason is that mutual funds are very heavily advertised, and almost everybody in the financial industry wants to sell you mutual funds.

Here we come to the most important question: "Why?" Why does the financial industry try so hard to sell you mutual funds?

By now you probably know the answer – because they make a lot of money. Mutual funds are one of the biggest money-makers for the financial industry, and investors all around the world don't even begin to imagine how much money is taken from them by the mutual fund industry.

It's not their fault. It's almost impossible for a person to understand the commission structure of mutual funds because of the Commission Camouflage Effect. I was fooled by it, too, at the start of my investing career. That is why, like millions of people all around the world, I invested most of my money in mutual funds. Now, let's take a look at why I sold all my mutual funds and put my money in a different financial product.

# Why so Many People Hate Investing?

The main reason why many people don't even want to think about investing, or even hate investing, is that the investing world is very hard to understand.

If you try to read some investing books, if you attend some investing seminars, or if you read some investing articles, you will be bombarded with words like: deferred sales charge, dynamic correlation, equity benchmarks, out-of-the-money put options, collateralized mortgage obligations, sovereign bonds, social impact bonds, leveraged index funds, weather derivatives, REITs, long-term equity anticipation securities, collateralized debt obligations...

Does your head hurt yet?

It's no wonder that people stay away from investing and give their money to financial advisers. I believe that this is done intentionally to make you think that you can't do it by yourself. So, you just give your money to somebody else to manage. When somebody else manages your money and investments, you can be sure that they will think about their own interests first. Remember: the person who controls the money wins!

So, let's take a closer look at how the financial industry rigged the long-term investing game in their favor, and why investors all over the world are losing most of the investing returns that should rightfully be theirs.

The tragic story starts with the commissions and fees that mutual funds charge. These commissions and fees seem very small, but, like I explained in the second chapter of this book, our brains are not equipped to understand their effects over long periods of time.

Let's take a look at them in a simplified way.

There are basically two types of commissions that mutual funds charge:

## 1. Commissions you pay when you buy a mutual fund

Technical terms: sales charge, sales load, front-end load

This is a one-time commission that you pay when you buy a mutual fund. For example, you invest $10,000 in a mutual fund that has a sales charge of 3%. The seller, in this case, takes 3% or $300 and your investment in the mutual fund after this cost is $9,700.

Sometimes, these commissions are not charged when you buy a mutual fund, but when you sell it. In that case, the commission is called a Deferred sales charge (back-end sales load). In this case, all of your money is immediately used to purchase fund shares. Commission is then deducted when you sell your fund shares.

## 2. Commissions you pay annually for the entire period of ownership of the fund.

Technical terms: Expense Ratio, Total Expense Ratio (TER) or Total Annual Operating Charges

To create maximum confusion among investors, there are all sorts of annual commissions and fees that mutual funds charge: Management fees, administrative fees, operating expenses, marketing expenses. You name it; it's there!

You won't believe it, but there is also a commission called the *invisible charge*. Do you remember the TV series Star Trek? In this series, human adversaries Klingons and Romulans could "cloak" their spaceships and thus render them invisible. It seems like the financial industry partnered with them to get this technology, so now "invisible" charges can add as much as 0.15% to a fund's annual expenses. Because of the cloaking device the financial industry employs, they are not included in a fund's expense ratio. Go figure.

Now, to make it simple, all these fees combined make up the annual charge that the company operating the fund takes out of your assets in the mutual fund every single year. But be careful! Keep in mind that the famous "management fee" is only a part of the annual costs. In the mutual fund prospectus, always check the Total Expense Ratio (TER) or Total Annual Operating Charges. This number is the sum of all the annual fees. For the sake of simplicity, I will refer to this cost as an expense ratio in the future.

The lower the number, the better off you are. The higher the number, the more money is transferred to the financial industry - and you keep less.

# "Investing is simple. It's the financial industry that works hard to make it complex!"

### @RobertRolih #MillionDollarDecision

Example: If the fund in which you invest has a 2.5% expense ratio, and the value of your assets in this fund is, on average, $10,000 during the last year, you would incur $250 in costs. And the story repeats every single year.

Here's the key: all the one-time commissions associated with mutual funds are pretty much not important. The annual commissions (expense ratio) that are taken every year are of enormous importance. Typically, they range between 1% and 3%.

Mutual funds in the U.S. charge approximately 1.25% annually, according to Morningstar. Add to that the invisible and hidden charges, and you end up with at least 2%, and, in some cases, even a 3% or 4% expense ratio. And for mutual funds based anywhere else in the world, these fees are, on average, slightly higher.

Now you are probably thinking… but these numbers are not so high. I can live with the financial industry taking 2% or 2.5% out of my assets every year. It's not such a bad deal.

But you forgot something. You forgot about the power of compound interest.

## *The Dark Side of Compounding*

When I told you the story about the magic rabbits, I used 100% growth as an example. But what if rabbits don't multiply so fast, and we only have 50% growth each year instead of 100%?

Let's check the numbers. For the sake of clarity, I removed the decimal places.

**Exhibit 5.4** Comparing 100% growth to 50% growth

| Days | Number of rabbits (100% growth) | Number of rabbits (50% growth) |
|---|---|---|
| 1 | 2 | 2 |
| 2 | 4 | 3 |
| 3 | 8 | 5 |
| 4 | 16 | 7 |
| 5 | 32 | 10 |
| 6 | 64 | 15 |
| 7 | 128 | 23 |
| 8 | 256 | 34 |
| 9 | 512 | 51 |
| 10 | 1,024 | 77 |
| ... | | |
| 20 | 1,048,576 | 4,434 |
| ... | | |
| 30 | 1,073,741,824 | 255,668 |
| ... | | |
| 33 | 8,589,934,592 | 862,880 |

As you can see, the differences are staggering. On day 10, you get 1,024 rabbits when you have 100% growth, and if you decrease it to 50%, you only get 77 rabbits.

On day 33, it's 862,880, instead of 8.5 billion. The growth was only halved, but you got 10,000 times fewer rabbits! A staggering difference. That is why I call this "The Dark Side of Compounding."

Ok, you saw how the change in the growth rate effects the procreation of rabbits. Now, it's time to get serious and check the same effect on your long-term investments.

First, we will check the best-case scenario of investing in a mutual fund that has a really low expense ratio of 1.25%. There are not many of them and if you invest in mutual funds, there is a very high probability that you are paying much more. For the sake of simplicity, we will use a one-time investment of $10,000 and assume a constant 10% annual growth of the market. Then, we will compare the growth of this investment if there were no commissions and if there was a 1.25% expense ratio.

**Exhibit 5.5** Effect of 1.25% annual fee on the growth of your investment

| Years | No commissions | 1.25% expense ratio |
|-------|----------------|---------------------|
| 0 | $10,000 | $10,000 |
| 1 | $11,000 | $10,875 |
| 2 | $12,100 | $11,827 |
| 3 | $13,310 | $12,861 |
| ... | | |
| 10 | $25,937 | $23,136 |
| ... | | |
| 20 | $67,275 | $53,529 |
| ... | | |
| 30 | $174,494 | $123,845 |

As you see in the table, in year 30, the difference is $50,649. That means that the 1.25% expense ratio takes away 30% of your money in the long run.

Like we said though, it's much more probable that your expense ratio when investing in mutual funds is closer to 2% or 2.5%. Let's take a look at what happens when you are investing in a mutual fund that has a 2.5% expense ratio.

**Exhibit 5.6** Effect of 2.5% expense ratio on the growth of your investment

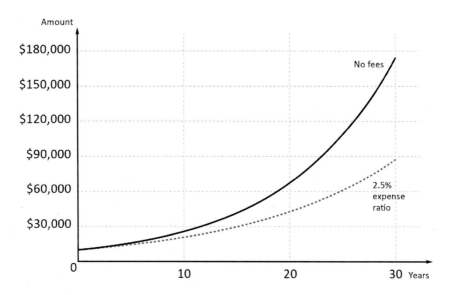

If the previous scenario shocked you, you probably can't even find words for this one. In that case, you are getting ripped off, as approximately half of your money disappears because of the commissions!

The companies that operate these mutual funds are taking staggering amounts of money from investors and destroying their financial future. People who invest in these kinds of mutual funds are leaving around 50% of their money on the table – the money that should be rightfully theirs.

From my experience, I can say with total confidence that most investors don't have a clue about these fees. Even if they are aware of them, they don't understand the real, long-term effects of the commissions on their investments.

At my seminars, I meet thousands of investors who are totally shocked when I show them these numbers. Usually, they just stare in disbelief.

A year ago, I had a seminar in Bucharest, Romania, and a lady in her 50's came to me during the break. She was very official looking with grey hair and glasses. She told me that 15 years ago, she invested more than €1m of her money in a Luxembourg based mutual fund, and that she just checked its expense ratio online. She was visibly distressed and she was almost stuttering when she told me that the expense ratio of her mutual fund was 2.7%.

Just a quick calculation can tell you that she lost a fortune by investing in a product that is probably a huge profit center for the company that operates it.

# "Even a 1% difference in expense ratio can make all the difference between a comfortable retirement and financial distress."

### @RobertRolih #MillionDollarDecision

If I summarize, mutual funds would be a great long-term investing product…that is, if they didn't have high commissions and fees that take away most of our potential returns. And now you are probably asking yourself if there is a financial product available that is similar, but without high commissions.

I have to disappoint you. There's not.

No, just kidding! We will take a look at this product in the next segment.

# *The Year that Changed It All*

Once upon a time, there was a man named John Bogle. He was born in 1929 in New Jersey, and attended Princeton University, where he studied economics and investment. He was determined to examine parts of the mutual fund industry that had not been analyzed before. When he got his first job at the then famous Wellington Fund, the manager quickly found out that John knew more about mutual funds than anyone in the world.

John knew about the fact that the financial industry takes enormous amounts of money from mutual fund investors through commissions and fees, but, unlike other people in the financial industry, that bothered him.

Now, let's go back in time to the year 1975, maybe the most important year in the history of investing. In the years before that, there were some attempts to find a solution for the extremely high fees that the mutual fund industry charged investors, but they were all targeted to institutional investors. Retail investors simply couldn't get in.

Then Mr. Bogle, who was tired of the fact that the financial industry took enormous fees from investors, came up with the solution that is very similar to a mutual fund with one big difference.

Mutual funds are a great product because they enable investors to invest in a lot of stocks at the same time, and thus lower the risk that the stock pickers are exposed to. But the problem is that they charge outrageous fees that wreak havoc in the long run. So, the challenge was how to create a product that would be similar to mutual funds, but with much lower fees. This type of product would work for the investor and not for the financial industry.

To lower the fees for investors, Bogle needed to lower the operating costs of a fund. Mutual funds have three major types of operating costs:

1. **Fund managers:** Mutual funds hire fund managers who select or pick the stocks that are then represented in the mutual fund. Usually, fund managers buy and sell a lot of stocks every year, because they think that they will find stocks that outperform the market that way. They are paid millions to do it. If we take into account what I said earlier about the predictive power of stock pickers, you can clearly see that these people are paid a fortune to gamble with their picks, and the end result is that, on average, they underperform the market.

2. **Sales force:** Companies operating mutual funds usually have an army of salesmen that sell them to investors. This army is very expensive.

3. **Marketing:** Mutual fund industry spends a lot of money on marketing. That is why you can see a lot of ads for different mutual funds on TV, in print and online.

To create a better financial product for investors, Bogle needed to drastically lower these costs. First, he got rid of the salesmen and most of the marketing costs. But who would buy this product without extensive sales and marketing efforts? The answer is financially literate investors who have done their homework.

Next, he got rid of the stock pickers – the fund managers. But who would pick the stocks then? The answer is nobody! His ingenious idea was to invest in ALL the stocks that are already on a well-known list. These lists are called stock indices (or sometimes indexes), like, for example, the Dow Jones index or S&P 500 index.

Let me explain what the stock indices are, if you are not familiar with the term. The standard definition of an index would just confuse you so I will give you a simpler one. Stock index is, simply, a number that measures the value of a large basket of stocks. For example, S&P 500 index represents 500 biggest stocks in the United States. If a stock index goes up by 2%, then that means the total value of the stocks which make up the index has gone up by 2% in value. Some stocks could have lost some value and some of them could have gained some value. But the total value of all the stocks combined has gone up 2%.

Because Bogle's product invested in all the stocks in a specific index, it was named "index fund" or "tracker fund" (because it tracks the performance of an index). This is the product that the financial industry would rather not tell you about. This product has very, very low fees. Because of the low fees, your money finally starts to work for you. You get to keep almost all of the future returns.

Let me simplify a little. An index fund is almost the same product as a mutual fund, but with much lower commissions. The typical index fund has an expense ratio of only 0.05% to 0.3%. That's a really low annual cost.

This product was first available to the general public in 1975. At that time the mutual fund industry labelled it "Bogle's folly" and even described it as "un-American". That was hardly a surprise, as index funds posed a great threat to its profits.

To really grasp the difference in the expense ratio among mutual funds and index funds, let's take a look at the comparison.

**Exhibit 5.7** Comparing different expense ratios

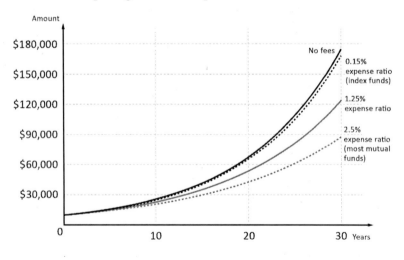

If you invested $10,000 in a typical mutual fund (2.5% expense ratio), you would end up with $87,550 in 30 years. But if you invested the same amount in a typical index fund, you would accumulate $167,495.

The difference is huge and could dramatically change the quality of life you will enjoy when you retire.

## You Can't Invest in Something if You Don't Know It Exists

The Investment Company Institute estimates that more than 54.9 million U.S. households own mutual funds (that is 43.6% of households) and only 5.9 million households own index funds[24]. Even though the number of people who invest in index funds is on the rise, mutual funds are still, by far, the most common type of fund owned by households.

It is hard to get reliable data on the index fund penetration rate in other countries, so I will make some estimates. One thing about which we can be certain is that the percentage of people who invest in index funds outside the United States is far lower than in the United States. BlackRock, for example, estimates that index funds currently represent only around 1% of investable assets in Europe.

In the last year, I have run a lot of seminars all around Europe, and my guestimate is similar to that of BlackRock. For example, when I ask people at my seminars in Europe to raise their hands if they know what mutual funds are, approximately 80% of the room raises their hands. When I ask about index funds, generally less than 5% of people know what they are.

So, why do so many people still invest in mutual funds, even though we can clearly see that mutual funds are just a weapon of financial self-destruction?

I think that there are several important reasons:

1. **People don't even know that index funds exist.** In my opinion, the financial industry tries hard to keep the information about index funds at bay. This is understandable – why would you talk about index funds when you can earn 5 or 10 times more money if you just sell mutual funds that are loaded with all sorts of fees? Keeping investors in the dark is good for business.

2. **Our brain is not equipped to understand the long-term effect of commissions.** Many investors are familiar with mutual funds and index funds, but they just don't understand the difference. Nobody explained to them the *Commission Camouflage Effect* and the *Dark Side of the Compounding*.

3. **People don't understand what index funds are.** At one of my workshops in London, I met a successful business owner who invests a lot of money in UK based mutual funds. He told me that he knew that index funds existed, but he never understood what they were and why they were better than mutual funds. He even tried to get some info online, but this info proved to be too technical and ambiguous. So, he just gave up and kept his money in mutual funds. That is until he attended my workshop.

4. **They think that the mutual fund they selected will outperform the market.** Yes, some investors think that they live in Lake Wobegon, "Where all the women are strong, all the men are good-looking and all the children are above average." It is a common misconception that you can beat the market if you just select the right mutual fund. The only problem is that the chances of doing so are far worse compared to winning big in Las Vegas.

   Allan S. Roth, the founder of Wealth Logic, ran thousands of simulations of investments in mutual funds and index funds over different periods of time. What he discovered is alarming for mutual fund investors. If you invest in mutual funds, your chances of beating passive index investing are dismal. If you invest in 5 different mutual funds, you only have a 1 in 33 chance of beating the index fund investor over the course of 25 years[25]. If you are more active as an investor, and you invest in 10 different mutual funds, you only have a 1 in 100 chance of success. Still want to bet your retirement pot? I recommend going to Las Vegas instead.

5.  **They just read an article about the next hot guru and want to invest in his fund, because he is a sure bet.** The only problem is that by the time somebody becomes famous, it's already too late, and you just get burned. There are hundreds of examples of this. Let me just give you one of them.

The well-known Magellan Fund reached its peak over the market in 1992. Between 1977 and 1990, the fund averaged a staggering 29% annual return under the management of the famous Peter Lynch. At that time, the fund attracted a huge mass of investors - they had assets of more than $100 billion. In the next 20 years, with all these investors on board, the fund started to fail. The returns the fund has now are quite terrible. In the last 10 years, the fund had a 5.6% annual return but the market had an 8.4% annual return. Now the fund has only 16 billion under management - down 84%.

Pay attention to what happened in this example, because this is one of the most reliable ways to lose money. When the fund was unknown, it had great returns. When it became famous, a lot of investors put their money in the fund. That means that they were too late. From then on, they only had below average returns.

Now you are probably thinking that you should have gotten on board sooner. The problem is that there are hundreds of funds that you could choose from and this one just got lucky. So you never know in advance which one out of the 100 funds will outperform the market in the short run. You can be quite sure that almost none of them will outperform the market in the long run. It's basic math.

# "Market returns, minus fees and commissions, are always less than the market returns."

### @RobertRolih #MillionDollarDecision

John C. Bogle said, "If you want to gamble with your retirement money, all I can say is be my guest, but be aware of the mathematical reality. The chances you will beat the market are infinitely small."

## *How to Beat Richard Branson with One Smart Move?*

To wrap up the chapter about long-term investing, I wanted to share with you a little-known fact that will probably surprise you. Especially if you are a business owner.

Have you heard of Richard Branson, the founder of the famous Virgin Group? If yes, you probably agree with me that he is one of the most successful business owners in the world. His results speak for themselves, and at the time of writing, Forbes estimates his net worth to $5 billion, putting him among the top 300 richest people in the world.

Branson's first successful company was Virgin Records, which he founded in 1972. The company became a worldwide success, issuing albums by artists like Mike Oldfield, the Spice Girls, Janet Jackson, Genesis, the Human League, Lenny Kravitz and others.

In 1992, Virgin suddenly struggled to stay financially afloat, and Branson sold it to Thorn EMI for a reported $1 billion in cash. One of the main reasons for doing so was that Branson wanted to invest money in his new business ventures and expand his Virgin Group. As we can see, he was very successful at doing that, as Virgin Group now consists of more than 400 companies worldwide.

But now prepare for a surprise.

If Richard Branson didn't invest the money he got from the Virgin Records sale into his own businesses, but into a simple index fund that tracked the performance of the 500 biggest U.S. companies (S&P 500), he would be worth $5.4bn at the time of writing this book. That is $400m more than the current estimate of his net worth.

If he invested that money in a technology index fund, he would be worth $8.8bn today.

Let me say this again. Richard Branson, one of the most successful entrepreneurs in the world, would be financially better off if he just invested his money in index funds and did nothing.

Of course, I'm not saying that in 1992 he should have invested all that money in index funds and retired to a tropical island. He would probably be bored to death in a couple of months, and his life would not leave a mark on this planet as it does now.

I'm just trying to show you how powerful it is investing in index funds. Even for successful business owners. The reality is that when you start your business, you can have huge growth rates in your business, year to year, but when your business matures, you can hardly keep up with the best companies in the world. Plus, your company, just like any other company, can get into financial trouble or even go out of business.

## "Even the most successful business owners in the world can hardly beat the returns of index funds."

### @RobertRolih #MillionDollarDecision

That is why it's not smart to only invest money in your business. I know a business owner who was very rich, but all of his money was in his own business. When the financial crisis hit, he lost a lot of customers and had to declare bankruptcy. He has not recovered since. So, even if you have a successful business, you need to invest a part of your profits in passive investments that take care of your safety and pension.

Let me summarize the chapter on long-term investing: compound interest is the most powerful concept you need to understand when investing for the long run. Unfortunately, there is also a dark side to it. That is why you can easily lose most of your future returns if you invest in the financial products that have high annual fees. Low cost investing products, like index funds, on the other hand, can be a real life-saver, as they channel the vast majority of the returns to the investor.

Before we dive into developing your investment strategy, let's take a look at another category of investments. This is short-term trading and investing. Short-term trading can be very lucrative, but also very dangerous. Let's check it out in the next chapter!

## *The Million Dollar Action Plan*

- Check the expense ratios of the funds that you own. If they are 0.5% or higher, replace them with index funds. We will talk about that in detail in the next chapters.

- Help your friends and business partners avoid the trap of investing in mutual funds and similar products. Share with them the message about the devastating effects of commissions on your investing returns. My designer has prepared some great infographics that you can share on social media right away. You can get them at www.MillionDollarDecisionBook.com/share

*"Our greatest fear should not be of failure, but of succeeding at things in life that don't really matter."*

– Francis Chan

# Chapter 6

---

## Short-Term Investing Slaughterhouse: Gurus on Hard Drugs Helping You to Part with Your Money

---

**O**ne of the most lucrative opportunities in the investing world is short-term trading. There are thousands of online brokers and so-called experts who want to teach you how to get amazing returns by trading stocks, options, commodities, currencies, cryptocurrencies, binary options and other financial instruments.

Then they add, "And all it takes is just a couple of minutes per day."

The prospect of becoming rich and financially free by trading is a very tempting proposition. It hits people straight in the limbic (emotional) part of the brain, bypassing the neocortex (thinking) part of the brain.

That is why many people start to trade with these instruments.

In this chapter, I will share with you what happens to them.

# "I Feel the Need, the Need for Speed!"

It's just an ordinary day at the office. You turn on your laptop and you scroll through your inbox. Spam, spam, spam…and, then, a subject captures your attention:

*"I Hope You're Sitting Down – how to give notice in one week."*

You open the message and you start to read…

*"Hi,*

*Imagine this for a moment… You open your trading account Monday morning, give notice at work on Friday, and then fly to Miami to board a cruise ship on Saturday.*

*Why not? You've made more than $50,000 your first week using (name of the service)!"*

You laugh, but it sounds really interesting. You click on the link and a website opens up.

The luxury boat is cruising near the coast of a tropical island. An attractive woman in a bikini drinks champagne. A person is driving a red Audi R8 on a beautiful scenic road. A good-looking couple swims in the pool.

You just ended up on a typical Forex broker webpage.

In the corner of the screen, you see a tagline: "Successful living starts with (name of the broker)," and you go, "Oh yes! This is the life I want to live!"

You scroll down… testimonials of people making a fortune with this platform, free training courses, award winning platform…

"Is this too good to be true?" your mind goes…

Hmmm…but all they are asking is $250 to start your journey to financial freedom and the lifestyle of your dreams. If you start with a $1,000 deposit, they will give you a whopping 50% bonus!

"It's just a small amount. What is the worst case scenario? I lose $1,000? No big deal," and you start to justify your decision.

Before you know it, you open an account and deposit $1,000.

The next day, you receive a phone call. It's Mr. Edward, your personal trading consultant. He is very professional, calm and gives you a sense of total confidence. He asks you about your goals and ambitions. He asks you about your trading experience. Then he goes on and starts to give you some trading tips and proposes that he opens some trades for you – with just $50. That's a very small amount and he sounds confident, so you give him a go.

The next day, you see all the trades in green, and you've earned $45. Wow! That's almost a 100% return on your investment!

Your phone rings again and it's Edward, your hero. After 10 minutes of discussion about the successful trades, he gives you an amazing offer. If you deposit another $5,000, he will give you a 100% deposit bonus and he will introduce you to some advanced strategies that can give you up to a 200% return on your money in just a month or two!

Now you are hooked! The luxury boat full of attractive women is within your grasp! You can smell it. Adrenaline starts to build and you are excited. You can see yourself earning tens of thousands… wait… hundreds of thousands of dollars almost overnight. You can hardly sleep at night from all the excitement.

$5,000 deposited. Plus, an additional $5,000 awarded to your account as a bonus. Ready, steady, go!

Edward shows you some great trading strategies, and you start to trade. Everything looks good. You open some trades and you get a nice return in just two days.

You start to get confident. You risk more and more, and then, after a week, it hits you. The first big loss. OK, nothing to worry about, says Edward. This happens to all of us, even the pros. You just need to follow the strategy and everything will be fine.

A month goes by and you are spending more and more time trading and analyzing charts. You seem not to be able to part from the computer for more than a few minutes. Bar charts are racing and your heart is racing, too. You suffer some more losses, but help is on the way.

Edward has some new strategies and invites you to join a $2,000 course where you will learn these strategies. "Yes, I need more training. I need more strategies if I want to achieve financial freedom."

At the course, you meet other people who are trading. There are also mentors, who boast about their results. You just need to keep trading. Practice makes perfect.

## "Easy money is never as easy as you thought at first."

### @RobertRolih #MillionDollarDecision

Six months go by. You are sitting in front of your laptop, and, as you check the account balance, the number is $1.73. You are defeated. All of your dreams of fast cars and beautiful women have faded away.

"Was Edward really Edward? Were the first trades he made real or just an artificially created illusion to get me hooked? Can I sue them?"

Now, that's a good idea! But your hopes of a big successful lawsuit disappear as soon as you take a look at their Terms & Conditions.

This was not a story I made up. This is a story that I hear over and over again from people all around the world.

It's a typical story of a regular guy turned Forex trader.

# *The Dreams They Promise & The Reality You Get*

It sounds easy. There are hundreds of Forex training companies and brokers that offer you Forex training, short-term stock trading training or options trading training and their promise goes something like this:

"Make 30% per year by learning these 3 simple strategies!" and most of the time they'll add, "Try it risk-free!"

Some "experts" in this industry, like Jose Tormos, even make claims like this[26]:

"It is (trading Forex) the easiest, most predictable and safest way to invest. You are missing out on opportunities to build a retirement nest egg."

Well, isn't that a really honest and realistic statement?

Or maybe he forgot to mention that retail Forex traders lose money most of the time, according to the industry's own data. Let's take a look at some interesting industry facts and statistics:

Recent reports from the two biggest publicly traded Forex companies (FXCM and Gain Capital Holdings) show that the vast majority of traders had a net loss from trading last year. At FXCM, 75% to 77% of customers lost money each quarter, according to newly required disclosures to the Commodity Futures Trading Commission[27]. At Gain Capital, the number of unprofitable customers hovered between 72% and 79% every quarter, according to its filing.

Also, this data needs to be corrected, because of the survivorship bias. Usually, the data they publish is only the data gathered from the active account holders. That means that every person who lost all money and closed his/her account is not accounted for anymore.

# "If you have a financial death wish... start trading!"

**@RobertRolih #MillionDollarDecision**

Furthermore, what these numbers don't show is the extent of profits and losses, and the losses are normally much higher than profits for short-term traders. That is why the Futures Association, an industry self-regulatory group, says that the average Forex trader loses all of his or her money and drops out of the market after just four months. To confirm that fact you can also check out FXCM's own statistics, that show that its customer turnover is about four times higher than that of an ordinary retail stock broker[28].

So, when you take a look at this statistic, you can easily calculate that it's not 70% to 80% of Forex traders who are losing their money; in reality, it's 95% or even more!

What about trading stocks for the short run? Do traders have more success there? Perhaps the most extensive study done in that area was published in 2011 by Barber, Lee, Liu and Odean. Using data from the Taiwanese Stock Exchange, the performance of day traders over the 15-year period 1992-2006 was evaluated[29].

The findings? The following statistics from their research paper "The Cross-Section of Speculator Skill: Evidence from Taiwan" is particularly revealing: In the average year, 360,000 individuals engaged in day trading. While about 87% had loses in the typical year, the results of their analysis suggest that less than 1,000 out of 360,000 traders were able to be profitable consistently. That is less than 0.2% of the traders. In other words, only two out of 1,000 stock traders could count on that source of income for their financial survival.

So much for the "most predictable and safest way to invest."

You could argue that only stock traders from Taiwan were somehow cursed with bad luck; but I have a feeling that the same curse is in effect all around the world.

In the last decade, I have read more than 300 books, thousands of articles and attended the best seminars on the topic of investing. I have spent more than $100,000 just for the seminar fees.

At first, when I still did not have a lot of knowledge about investing, I believed every word the "experts" at these seminars told me.

But, as the years went by and my financial education went up, I started to realize that most of the "experts" were just salesmen. They cared about one thing only: how to sell their product - and that product was usually a financial catastrophe for the customers.

Let me give you an example: at one of the seminars, the speaker was recommending short-term trading with financial instruments, like stocks and currencies, and he charged almost $5,000 for the course.

What he failed to mention was that in order to execute his strategies, you would need to pay an additional fee for the trading software and other services you needed. You would also need to sit in front of the computer screen for hours every day watching boring charts (and go nuts during every swing in price), and that 95% of his clients lost all of their money (as you would find out later when you talk with the participants in your group).

There were some people who had some gains, but they could barely cover the costs of running their "amazingly profitable trading business" with them. And they had not even accounted for the time spent in the process. Like I said before, time is money.

I have yet to find a short-term trader who accounts for his time spent for trading when calculating his Return on Investment (ROI). Like I explained in the chapter 2, time is a crucial ingredient of the real ROI calculation and can make a big difference in the resulting return.

## "Short-term trading is very time-consuming. That is why even "successful" short-term traders can easily have negative real ROI."

@RobertRolih #MillionDollarDecision

At one of my courses, there was a very interesting person, let's call him Charles. He approached me during the lunch break and said that he was making a lot of money trading Forex. He was very happy with his results and he couldn't stop boasting about his winning trades.

Then I asked him if we could calculate his real ROI, including time spent for trading. He agreed, and we put some numbers on a piece of paper.

He told me that he traded for at least three hours per day, almost every day. During the weekends, he was going through investing websites, preparing the trades for the following week and reading trading books.

So, an additional two to four hours every weekend. All together this accounted for approximately 950 hours of his time per year.

Then I asked him what was his personal income. It was around $70,000. We divided that by 1,800 working hours per year and found out that the value of one hour of his time was $39.

That meant that the cost of his time spent for trading was $36,944 (950 times 39).

I just can't forget the look on his face when we calculated that and saw that his real ROI was, in fact, deeply in the red. Surprise, surprise!!! He was working hard to lose money.

That's the story with most of the "successful" short-term traders. They never account for their time when they are doing the ROI calculations. They never ask themselves how much they would earn if they just invested the same amount of time to work in their business or to learn new money making skills, or how much happier they would be if they spent their time with their family.

## Zero Minus Two Equals Minus Two

Trading currencies, binary options, stocks, futures and any other short-term trading is a zero sum game. This means that when somebody wins, somebody else has to lose. All the profits that one trader earns, are taken from somebody else.

This is unlike investing in the stock market for the long run. Stocks are going up over time, because the companies, on average, are growing, increasing their profits, innovating and providing more value. That is why the S&P 500 went from 450 in 1995 to 2,200 in 2017, for example.

But when you invest in EUR/USD, for example, this currency pair is not providing any additional value. It doesn't grow. This is just an exchange rate. That is why EUR/USD exchange rate doesn't grow but oscillates between 1.00 and 1.50 over time.

If someone buys the EUR/USD currency pair, somebody else has to sell it. They both think they are smart and hope they will win, but one of them will lose. There is no other way.

From that we can deduct that, on average, nobody is a winner trading in the short run. But... we forgot to account for something very important, and these are the commissions and fees.

When you are trading, your broker takes a commission for every trade you place. Plus, there are additional overnight commissions that some brokers charge, withdrawal fees, and so on.

That means that short-term trading is not a zero-sum game, but a minus 2% to minus 5% sum game when you account for these commissions and fees. And, of course, the only winners in this game are a few professionals and some large financial institutions who can afford very expensive equipment to execute thousands, or even millions, of trades, a couple of nanoseconds before others can even think about it. For more information on that subject that probably costs retail traders billions of dollars per year, read the book *Flash Boys: A Wall Street Revolt* by Michael Lewis.

Am I saying that an average person can't be successful at short-term trading? No. There are some people who eventually succeed and become professionals. When you talk to them, you see that they needed to spend at least five years full-time trading before they became successful. The most important of all – they needed to have what I call "robot psychology." This means that they had an "accountant type" of personality where almost nothing could affect their emotions when trading.

When you draw the line, you can see that the problem is that there are very few of these professionals. From the stats I showed you, we can clearly see that much less than 1% of short-term traders become professionals who can make a living with trading, and that the average Forex trader loses all of his or her money and drops out of the market after just four months. That makes this Money Making activity pretty unattractive. Let me just compare it to starting a business.

According to the U.S. Bureau of Labor Statistics, 56% of small businesses survive 5 years, and 36% survive 10 years in business[30]. That means that you are at least 30 to 50 times more likely to succeed in business, compared to short-term trading. A huge difference.

# "You have 30 to 50 times better chances of creating a successful business than at succeeding as a short-term trader."

@RobertRolih #MillionDollarDecision

In my opinion, the main reason for this is that when you start a business, you are playing a non-zero-sum game. In other words, when you are growing your business, you are building new value. A value that didn't exist before. A value that is not taken from somebody else.

When you are trading, you are playing a worse than a zero-sum game. On top of that, you are not building any value.

That is why, in my opinion, short-term trading is just another tool that the financial industry uses to squeeze money out of your pocket. It's a giant tool that sucks money out of the masses and puts this money in the hands of big financial institutions.

That is why Larry Harris, a USC professor and the former chief economist at the Securities and Exchange Commission said, "The business model for Forex trading is to burn the customer and then find another one."

## *The Quickest Way to a Mental Hospital*

I just spoke to one of the bad guys of the financial industry. A Forex trading "guru."

I don't get along well with short-term trading "gurus," because what I teach is not good for their business. During our conversation, I told him that I would not recommend his courses to my customers, because Forex trading was a losing proposition from the start, and the only ones that were winning the game were the brokers, a few other financial institutions and gurus teaching people how to trade (like him).

His reply was: "Yes, but at least people can get mentally stronger when they trade Forex, and even if they lose money, this can help them in their jobs or in their business."

Hmmm… isn't that a nice way to justify your actions!

Now, let's take a closer look at that statement. Is trading really good for developing a stronger mentality?

I tend to disagree. Why? Mostly because more than 19 out of 20 people fail at trading. Even after they invested in courses, spent months practicing it and tried different systems of trading, they still fail. After they try again, they still fail, and after years of trying again and learning, they still fail. There is no way out.

That makes a mess in your brain regarding a very useful law that rules our lives. I'm talking about the law of cause and effect. Usually in life, when we train and work hard, we see improvement; we see that our results get better and better. So, you have this great feedback loop where the more effort you put in, the better you become. This motivates you to do your best and to work hard, because you know that you will be rewarded for your effort. You see gradual improvement along the way.

In the short-term trading space, I saw hundreds of people who did that, and their results only got worse. So, how can that make you mentally strong? Quite the opposite; it makes you a nervous wreck that could quickly end up in a mental hospital, and you start thinking that whatever you do, you will never succeed.

If you fail in business, you at least get some business experience and business skills out of that. So, in your next venture, your chances of success are higher. The only thing you get from learning to trade is disappointment and low self-esteem. Plus, you start to think that you are not in control, that external forces rule your life.

Another thing that most people don't think about when they start trading is that trading is a totally self-centered activity. Trading doesn't help anyone. Nobody's life gets better because you do it, especially not yours when you lose your money. You are not making this planet or your community a better place by doing it.

## "Trading the markets is a totally self-centered activity. Nobody's life gets better because you trade. Except your broker's life."

@RobertRolih #MillionDollarDecision

Many studies have shown that being of use, or helping others, is one of the key ingredients for happiness in life. Humans evolved as compassionate creatures, and that enabled us to survive and to evolve. That is why your brain releases feel-good chemicals when you are helping others. It's an evolutionary mechanism. If you are positively impacting other people, for example, at your job or in your business, you are simply happier. You have more self-esteem, your self-worth increases and your overall well-being increases. Helping others releases endorphins in the brain, and can also produce the positive feeling known as the "helper's high."

To summarize, you will be much happier (and richer), if you just leave trading alone.

But what about automated systems for trading? Wouldn't that solve the problem of time? Let's take a look.

## *Automated Systems for Losing Money*

"Just relax and watch our automated trading system make money for you! Guaranteed!"

"Earn $3,000 a week trading commodities without lifting a finger. Your financial freedom is now within reach with [system name]!"

Now and then, somebody asks me a question about automated trading systems or algorithmic trading. These are computer-based trading applications that are set up to automatically buy and sell financial instruments on your behalf.

Imagine this: you subscribe to an automated trading service and fund your account. From then on, everything is automated. You can go to the beach and enjoy yourself, while the automated trading system works day and night and makes money for you.

The best thing of all, you can buy one for just $200. Some companies even offer them for free. A few days ago, I saw an interesting ad online. It said, "How I make $3,000 per day trading."

I just love to check out this kind of ads. You can always get a good laugh. With that one, I just couldn't stop laughing when I watched the video on the website.

It starts with a beautiful woman in her 40's, driving a Jaguar, telling people how she makes a ton of money from home. Then she parks the car in front of a big, luxury mansion and goes in. She sits on a sofa and starts to describe how her late husband, who was employed in the secret service, gave her the secret technology that predicts the movements of the Forex markets.

Because she is such a good soul, she already shared it with some of her friends, and now they are all insanely rich, driving sports cars and drinking champagne. The technology is so amazing that you don't even need to know how to use a computer to use it, as it does all the trading automatically for you.

Then comes the big revelation. Because she wants to help as many people as possible to become rich, she offers this technology for free. You just have to open an account and fund it with $1,000 on her platform. Wow! She has the most powerful technology that predicts the future and you will get it for free.

I just couldn't stop laughing. The person who wrote the scenario for that video should be hired in Hollywood for making sitcoms.

Some people obviously make the investment. The typical customer is, of course, a young male, dreaming of all the hot girls that will be attracted to him when he is driving around in his red Ferrari convertible.

But in reality, the only thing automated trading does is drain your account, and it does that very efficiently. The only people making money with automated systems of trading are the big financial institutions, who probably work with systems worth hundreds of millions of dollars and have the fastest connections to the stock exchanges. Sophisticated systems, plus a couple of nanoseconds advantage, gives them an edge and that is all they need to make money.

Thinking that something like this would be available to the retail customers for a couple of hundred dollars is a serious delusion.

So, when somebody approaches you and offers you their new trading software, ask them why they are not on a tropical island living happily ever after.

# *Let's Help Africa by Teaching Young Boys to Trade Forex*

My aim for this chapter was to turn you away from short-term trading. It's only good for the financial industry and not for you. If I was successful at that, you just saved a lot of money and time.

If you think that you have too much money, and you are looking for a way to get rid of it, don't trade. Give your money to a charity instead, or, if that doesn't work for you, you can wire the money to me.

Let me end this chapter with a personal story. In the past, I was also one of the people who traded stocks and Forex. I lost a lot of money and I almost broke my marriage in the process. Yes, I admit it. I was young and foolish.

It all began when I listened to a presentation by a famous Forex guru who owned a company that offered Forex courses. The presentation blew me away. What it said was something like this:

"I can teach you 3 strategies for trading Forex that will enable you to get at least 30% return on your money every year, and you need only two hours per week to do it. It's so simple that even my 9-year-old kid does it."

After the first course, there was another course, and after that, there was a one-year program promising unlimited wealth. Altogether, I spent $23,000 for courses with this company. In my group, there were around 40 people like me. After two years of learning and trading, the only thing I had to show was huge losses.

So, I started to ask other people in the course about their results. Surprise, surprise, I was not the only one with this kind of result. Soon, I found out that only one person in the group made a profit. All the rest had losses.

After that, I came to my senses and I promised myself never to trade Forex or any other short-term products anymore. Enough is enough.

Now, that could be the end of my story. But, just a couple of months ago, I read something very interesting and somewhat disturbing.

The Forex guru, whose courses I attended, is said to be a hard drugs user and needs to pay strippers to come to his birthday party because his friends won't come. In addition to that, he now has a very bad reputation. Ripping people off eventually catches up with you. So, now he runs his Forex courses mainly in Africa. Young African boys are running to the back of the rooms to sign up for his courses.

I guess this is his way of helping to fight poverty in Africa.

In summary: some battles are just not worth fighting, and short-term trading is definitely one of them. The chances of winning this game are next to none and not worth the risk. Now that you know the key principles of long-term and short-term investing, it's time to create your investing strategy. Let's do it in the next chapter.

## *The Million Dollar Action Plan*

- If you are trading the markets, stop. Spend your time in Money Making activities instead. And don't forget to thank me later.

- Share the message about the dangers of short-term trading with your friends. The online world is filled with misleading ads and promises about that topic. My designer prepared an amazing explainer video that you can share on social media right away. You can get it at www.MillionDollarDecisionBook.com/share. By sharing it, you could easily save the financial lives of many people.

*"Wealth is the product of a man's capacity to think."*

– Ayn Rand

# Chapter 7

---

## Fast Forward >> The Simple Way to Win the Financial Game of Life

---

One of the most important things I learned in life is the importance of having a strategy.

Having a strategy means that you have a plan designed to achieve your long-term goals or vision.

Most people don't have this kind of plan, and, even worse, most people don't even have a clear vision of what they want to achieve in the next 10 or 20 years. If you don't have your own goals and vision, you will always work hard to make somebody else's vision a reality. As a result of that, your financial rewards will always be average – just enough to get by and to live an unfulfilled life full of worry.

That is why I believe that the most valuable activity you can undertake every day is called thinking. You see, thinking about what you want to achieve and how to achieve it is something that makes a difference between living a mediocre life and an extraordinary life.

Just by thinking about these two things, a person of average intelligence and talent can be much more successful than his superiorly gifted peers. I believe that success in life is not the result of intelligence, but using what you have been given to know where you are going, and having a plan to get there and then taking the action to complete it.

In this chapter, I will help you take everything you have learned so far and create a strategy to win the financial game of life.

By now, you should have the right philosophy, or way of thinking, about all your Money Making and Investing activities that are encompassed in the Financial Success Formula™. Now, it's time to go to the drawing board and create a battle plan.

## *Your Million Dollar Decision*

The title of this book could seem a bit exaggerated at first sight. But, as you saw, the amount of money that investors lose because of the way the financial industry operates and the way our brains work is simply staggering.

This book is all about the Million Dollar Decision you need to make when investing. Most people take the wrong turn here, and they trust the financial industry that makes that decision for them.

Let me show you how easily that decision can amount to one million dollars over the investing career of an average U.S. family.

Joe and Mary are an average middle-class family with two kids, and they live a pretty normal life. They know that they need to invest, and they trust their financial adviser to make the key investing decisions for them. After all, he is a very nice guy who wouldn't hurt a fly.

What they don't understand is that the decision to trust their adviser and the financial industry will cost them an arm and a leg. And there is a good chance that even their financial adviser doesn't have the slightest idea that his recommendations will cut Joe and Mary's retirement pot in half.

So, let's do a quick calculation and check what will happen with their investments.

According to the U.S. Census Bureau, the average U.S. household income was $73,298 in 2014[31]. Let's round that down to $70,000, and I will also not adjust for inflation in this example, just for the sake of clarity.

Let's assume that they invest just 10% of that income each year in order to secure a safe financial future and finance their pensions. Let's say that they start doing that at the age of 30, and they keep doing it till they retire at the age of 70 (much more realistic nowadays than 65.) That's 40 years.

When calculating the returns, I will use 8% as the average annual growth of the market. That is 2 percentage points lower than the historical average for stocks.

$7,000 invested annually, growing at 8% annually for 40 years amounts to $2,110,539.

But hey, didn't we forget something?

Yes, we did! Because they trust their adviser, who recommends investing in mutual funds, and that the financial industry will take 2% of their assets annually. That means that they will not end up with $2,110,539, but only $1,220,334.

## MONEY ACCUMULATED IN 40 YEARS

IF THERE WERE NO COMMISSIONS

$2,110,539

MUTUAL FUNDS

$1,220,334

## DIFFERENCE : $890,205

That's $890,205 less money! Looks like the dark side of compounding took almost half of their retirement pot.

But, like we said also, investing in index funds is not free. So, let's say that instead of choosing mutual funds, they read this book, and they invested in index funds with 0.2% expense ratio.

That would give them $1,995,979 in 40 years.

## MONEY ACCUMULATED IN 40 YEARS: COMPARING MUTUAL AND INDEX FUNDS

IN INDEX FUNDS

$1,995,979

IN MUTUAL FUNDS

$1,220,334

## DIFFERENCE : $775,645

So, the real difference between investing in mutual funds and index funds would be $775,645. That's a lot of money. This difference could mean the difference between a nice and safe retirement, and financial worries in their senior years.

Now, let's further assume that Joe (it's always the man) fell prey to one of the short-term investing gurus, and started to trade Forex for a couple of years when he was 32 years old. He spent $5,000 for the courses, and he lost another $10,000 when trading. Then, his wife found out what was going on and threatened to divorce him if he didn't stop.

Joe came to his senses, and he only lost $15,000.

A simple calculation can tell you that if they just invested that lost money into a simple index fund for 38 years, they would have $260,378 more in their investing account when they retired at 70. And I didn't even account for the value of the time spent trading Forex and the opportunity costs.

Let's sum up these numbers:

## HOW TO SAVE A MILLION DOLLARS?

DIFFERENCE FROM LONG-TERM INVESTMENTS: **$775,645**

DIFFERENCE FROM SHORT-TERM INVESTMENTS: **$260,378**

TOTAL: **$1,036,023**

Long-term investing losses ($775,645), plus short-term trading losses ($260,378), equals $1,036,023.

That is why the title of this book is *The Million Dollar Decision*. The simple fact is that an average family with an average income can easily lose more than one million dollars if they fall prey to the financial industry's claws. The sad thing is most families do.

You, on the other hand, are now prepared to make the right decision that will enable you to save at least one million dollars in the future.

## *Peel Bananas the Right Way, and Start Your Investing Revolution*

A while ago, I came across a short video clip on Facebook about a very interesting life hack. The clip said that most of us have been taught to peel bananas the wrong way. Because my family eats quite a lot of bananas, and sometimes they are quite hard to peel, I checked out the video.

In the video, there was a funny guy wearing monkey underwear who said that monkeys are the real masters of peeling bananas (looks like we can learn much more than stock picking from monkeys.) Then, he demonstrated how they do it. When a monkey wants to peel the banana, he puts it upside down, and then pinches the tip between his thumb and forefingers. That splits the skin swiftly into two segments, and makes peeling easy - and bruise-free.

After I watched that video, I thought: "I have been peeling bananas the hard way my whole life! This solution is so simple; why didn't I think of it?"

The truth is that simple solutions are usually the best solutions. Most of the time it's very difficult to find this kind of solution in our information overloaded world.

That is why Steve Jobs said that, "Simple can be harder than complex: You have to work hard to get your thinking clean to make it simple. But, it's worth it in the end, because once you get there, you can move mountains."

# "Simple solutions are usually the best solutions. But most of the time it's hard to find them."

### @RobertRolih #MillionDollarDecision

To find simple solutions that I shared with you, I needed years and years of hard work. I lost a lot of money in the process and I needed to think very hard how to simplify everything to the point that a person who hates investing mumbo jumbo understands it. At least I hope I have done so.

I also hope that, by now, you understand why the investing world is so complicated. There is a lot of money to be made by the people who complicate it. As a result of that, the people in the financial industry will tell you that you can't do it by yourself, and that you need a financial adviser.

But I believe that, with the right knowledge, you can do it by yourself in no time and save a million in the process.

In the end, the only way you can win the investing game is to simplify it. When you have won the game, you realize that simplicity is the ultimate sophistication, if I quote Leonardo da Vinci correctly.

## *Financial Freedom in A Couple of Hours per Year*

To learn any new skill, like selling, playing piano, using Photoshop or singing, you need time. The more time you invest in learning and practicing that skill, the better you become.

Scientists maintain that for many complex skills, you need 10,000 hours, or 10 years of your life, if you want to master them and become one of the best in the world at that skill[32]. Hard work and single-minded focus produces exceptional results. All the top athletes, business owners, entertainers or artists know that. That is why they are amongst the top earners in their fields.

It seems logical that the same rule should apply to investing. The more time and effort we put in, the better returns we should get.

**Exhibit 7.1** How we tend to think about investing (the typical learning curve)

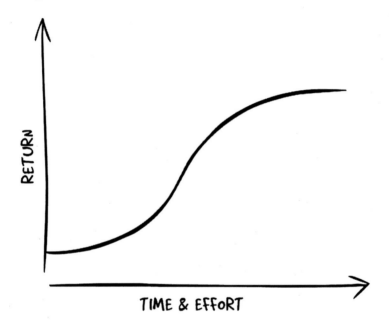

But I believe that, in the world of investing, this logic doesn't work and can only bring you financial hardship.

I think that the world of investing follows a completely different logic. If you do nothing, and just trust your financial adviser, you will have mediocre returns minus commissions. If you spend some time to learn the right details, and employ passive investing strategies from this book, without even touching the short-term trading world, you get great returns.

Then, if you start to invest more time and effort into investing, trading and learning how to pick stocks, you will start to get disappointing returns. The usual logic breaks down here, and even if you put in more time, your returns don't go up.

**Exhibit 7.2** How it works in real life – the distorted learning curve

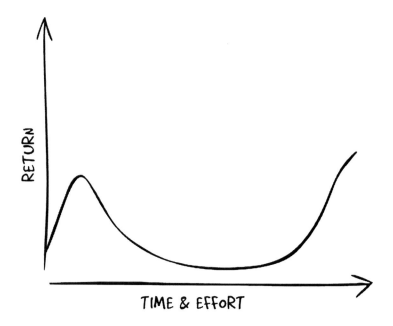

Only if you devote your whole life to investing, like Warren Buffett, for example, can you expect your returns to go up. But think about it: is it worth it? Is it worth it to spend your life watching the charts, analyzing balance sheets and reading corporate reports?

Well, if that is your thing, give it a shot; but, for most people - me included - these things are boring. I bet that when you are on your deathbed, you will not say: "Uh, I wish I spent more time looking at stock charts and corporate reports."

Apart from that, you are not adding any value to this world if you are just investing your money in different stocks and other instruments.

# "When investing, more effort means worse results, most of the time."

**@RobertRolih #MillionDollarDecision**

But in the previous two charts, we forgot to account for one important thing: time. Like we already established, time is money. When you account for the value of time invested, you get a chart like the one below, with most investors producing negative returns.

**Exhibit 7.3** The distorted learning curve accounting for the value of time (dotted line)

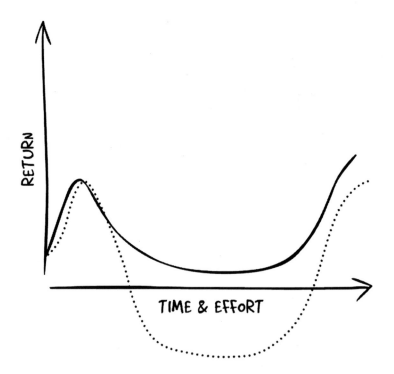

Even educated investors, who spend just a couple of hours investing, can compete with most investors who devote their lives to investing.

When you are thinking about your strategy to win the financial game of life, remember one thing. It's very important to decide what you will do in your Money Making and Investing activities.

But it could be even more important to decide what you will not do. Which activities you will not conduct.

Michael Porter, a famous economist, said, "The essence of strategy is choosing what not to do." In investing, and in business, you can achieve much more by simply saying NO to some opportunities or activities. The Financial industry would love you to trade Forex, read the financial news every day, pick stocks and go nuts with every price move, speculate with options and so on.

But I believe that to financially succeed in life, it's much better to say NO to these things and to spend your time learning business and other Money Making skills.

In the Financial Success Formula™, this means being very active and aggressive in the Money Making part of the equation, and passive and careful in the Investing part of the formula.

NO can be the most powerful word in your financial life. Use it often!

## *Your Investing Masterplan*

This is where the rubber meets the road. Let's create a simple investing master plan that will provide you with the best possible investing returns, and peace of mind.

If you are a non-U.S. resident, please note that there are some specifics you need to know about the products and the companies I talk about in this section. Please visit www.MillionDollarDecisionBook.com/bonus for more information.

First, let's choose the investing vehicle. There are many options on the market. We already concluded that we don't want financial advisers or wealth managers putting their greedy fingers into our investment portfolio. What about using increasingly popular robo-advisors, or target date retirement funds?

First let's take a look at target date retirement funds, also known as a lifecycle, dynamic-risk or age-based funds. These funds are being professionally managed to meet the needs of someone planning to retire near the calendar year that appears in the name of the fund. The fund adjusts its asset allocation model, as it gets closer to that year making it increasingly more conservative by investing a larger proportion of the fund in bonds.

Target date retirement funds are a good option if you are not prepared to invest a couple of hours into your investing education. As you already did that by reading this book, you can easily bypass them. There are two problems when investing for retirement that way:

- Their costs can be quite high. Most of them have expense ratios from 0.10% to 1.00%. If you own one that has 0.10% expense ratio, it's OK, but anything over 0.30% can be a real money drain over the long run, like we have discussed many times already.

- They don't take into account what your investing goals are, how much you are saving, what assets you own elsewhere, if you will have other income sources in retirement, or what your risk tolerance is…and these are very important questions.

What about robo-advisors? Robo-advisors are an online portfolio management service that provides automated, algorithm-based investing advice without the use of human financial planners. They have lower fees compared to target date retirement funds, making them an interesting choice with only a few drawbacks that include:

- They only offer a one-size-fits-all solution and doesn't allow for some flexibility.

- Even though they have very low fees, these fees, over time, can cost you a substantial amount of money.

That is why instead of all these options, I recommend you use a low-cost investing company like Vanguard (www.vanguard.com) or Fidelity (www.fidelity.com) that will take care of your IRA or plain investment account. This guarantees you the lowest possible costs, and thus the highest possible future returns. Plus, it gives you the additional flexibility that all the other options lack.

The core of your portfolio should be composed of three components:

## 1. U.S. stocks

The first component is the exposure to the entire U.S. stock market, including companies with a relatively small market capitalization (technical term for that is small-cap). This is very important because small-cap stocks have more room to grow, and they usually outperform large-cap stocks over the long run.

## 2. International stocks

For the second part of your investment money, most experts tell you to choose a basket of international stocks (total International stock funds), but that is a very poor choice. Instead, I invest in emerging markets stock funds. Why? If you take a closer look at any international stock fund, you will see that it invests mostly in companies from Europe, Australia and Japan. If you ask yourself what kind of growth potential is there, you can easily answer "very limited." In simple terms, emerging markets offer you a much greater growth perspective. They have outperformed Europe, Australia, and Japan in the last decade by 40 percentage points and even though you can never make predictions based on past returns, they are almost certainly a much better choice for the long run.

## 3. Bonds

The third part of your money should go into bonds. Bonds are very important when you get older, because they provide stability and safety when markets turn volatile.

So, that is the core of your portfolio. The basic guideline is to weigh your portfolio heavily towards stocks when you are younger, and make it increasingly more conservative as your retirement age comes closer.

Now you are probably asking yourself which low-cost investing company to use and which specific funds to choose. To help you with that I prepared a special section on The Million Dollar Decision members-only website. To get access, visit www.MillionDollarDecisionBook.com/bonus.

## *Warren Buffett, Mike Tyson and You*

"How beautiful! How beautiful! How beautiful!" whispers Rupert, my four-year-old son. Two-year-old Rafael is quieter and just stares in amazement. After all, he doesn't know the words to express what he feels yet.

It's December 2015. We just landed on Mahé Island, Seychelles, and we are driving towards our hotel. My wife Sara and I look at each other, smiling, enjoying the moment. The scene is fantastic.

We are driving up the hill on this tropical island. There is a jungle with beautiful trees all around us. There are rounded dark brown cliffs in the distance. When you look towards the ocean, you see a beautiful bay with crystal clear water and a tropical beach. Paradise.

It's moments like this that stay with you forever.

When I was young, I couldn't even dream about the life I live right now with my family. My parents were poor as church mice, I had no special talents, I was average in school and I only started to learn to speak English when I was a teenager. So, if you were a neutral observer at that time, you would say that I would never amount to anything.

But I had something that changed that fate, and that was the vision where I saw myself as a successful business owner in the future. As a teenager, I would go to the library in town and borrow business books. My favorite author was Brian Tracy. I would read these books about goal setting and business skills for hours and hours.

So, in 2001, when I was a student living in a student dorm, an opportunity presented itself and I started my company from zero. Well, it was not exactly zero. You see, I had two very big advantages over other business owners. The first one was a phone – a landline that was present in all the rooms in the student dorm. The second one was an old personal computer that barely worked.

As luck would have it, my business grew, and in my late 20s, I made my first six-figure income. They say that money is not everything, and I agree, but I also know that I would not have visited Seychelles and hundreds of other amazing places with my family if I didn't have the money. I know that when I didn't have money, I had more problems and worries about the future. I know that when I didn't have money, I had much less freedom.

# "They say money can't buy happiness. But it can sure as hell solve a lot of problems!"

### @RobertRolih #MillionDollarDecision

Let's face it: money is important in life. That is why you should take extra special care of it. After you have earned it, be very careful how much of it you spend and how you invest the rest.

If I summarize this book in a couple of sentences, it would go like this: life is too short to spend it looking at charts and financial news. Active investing doesn't add value to your life, nor does it make this world a better place. On top of that, it will not even give you better returns compared to passive investing. Quite the contrary – active investing will most likely ruin your financial life, and make you a nervous wreck. So, spend a couple of hours per year on investing with my system; be a passive investor.

With all the time you saved, focus on learning money making skills. In my opinion, the most powerful money making skills are business skills. These skills enable you to start your business and grow it profitably. Most millionaires alive today became rich through business. There are very few people who did it through investing alone.

Most of all, don't be frugal like Warren Buffett, who saves every little penny, still lives in the same house he bought in 1958, eats McDonald's hamburgers (one of the unhealthiest things you can eat) and drinks Coke (tons of sugar doesn't help you, either)[33].

On the other hand, don't spend all your money as soon as you have earned it, like Mike Tyson.

I think that going to extremes like that is not a good way to live.

My philosophy is to be somewhere in the middle. It's healthier, it's sustainable and it's fun. Having billions and never buying something nice gets boring and queer. On the other hand, Mike Tyson recklessness can burn your money quick, as it did for Tyson who ended up $38 million in debt.

So, don't go on a shopping spree when you increase your income, but invest a part of that money in passive investments, and buy some nice things or experiences with the rest. You only have one life to live. Do something good with it and have some fun!

**Exhibit 7.4** The two extremes of managing your money

WARREN BUFFETT FRUGAL

SAVE EVERY PENNY
EAT CHEAP & UNHEALTHY FOOD
NEVER TAKE A VACATION
NEVER BUY NICE THINGS
STAY IN A DIRT CHEAP APARTMENT
INVEST EVERY SINGLE DOLLAR YOU EARN

MIKE TYSON RECKLESS

BUY TENS OF SUPERCARS
EAT AT THE MOST EXPENSIVE RESTAURANTS
PARTY ALL THE TIME
GO ON A SHOPPING SPREE THAT NEVER STOPS
LIVE IN A LAVISH MANSION
INVEST NOTHING

## *You Can Make this World a Better Place Right Now*

You can smile now and shout (or maybe just whisper), "I did it!" knowing that we have reached the **beginning** of our journey. And no, there is no mistake. Although we have reached the end of this book, the real journey for you is just starting. It's time for you to invest using the strategies where YOU keep most of the future returns and not the financial industry.

Plus, it's time for you to make more money because, if you are like me, you want to get rich while you can still enjoy it.

To congratulate you, I prepared some valuable additional resources on Investing and Money Making that are a crucial part of the journey towards your financial goals and includes:

- The BONUS chapter *My Three Best Financial Breakthrough Cheat Codes.* This chapter is focused on three amazing strategies you can use to drastically increase your income. And no, it's not about "the usual stuff," like goal setting and positive thinking. These are little-known strategies that you can apply, right away, to make a quantum leap in your life.

- The seven best strategies for increasing income I learned from Brian Tracy.

- A list of the key questions to ask your insurance agent when you are buying different types of insurance policies.

- Step-by-step instructions on how and where to buy gold and silver. Plus, how to avoid the biggest mistakes people make when buying these precious metals.

- A guide to selecting a low-cost investing company and the specific index funds to use.

- A complimentary subscription to my *Million Dollar Strategies Newsletter*, with investing and money making tips.

- And much more…

If you haven't already registered for all these bonuses, do it now at www.MillionDollarDecisionBook.com/bonus

## *Do you consider yourself a helpful person?*

If you found this book useful, I would like to ask you a favor. Can you please help me make this world a better place by buying 20 copies of this book and giving them to your friends?

Just kidding!

All I ask you to do is to recommend this book to your friends. You can easily share explainer videos, infographics and quotes from this book here: www.MillionDollarDecisionBook.com/share

Plus, I would be eternally grateful, if you could **write an unbiased review of this book on Amazon.com.** This will help other people decide to get this book and save a ton of money. The financial industry is trying hard to keep this knowledge secret. When each one of us does something to spread the word, we are all making a big difference…a million-dollar difference in people's lives.

And it all starts with you.

I wish you all the success and freedom you can dream of,

Robert Rolih

P.S. When you register for the bonuses, you will start receiving my *Million Dollar Strategies Newsletter*, where I share important updates, tips and strategies. I will not flood your inbox with irrelevant stuff – I will only write to you when I have something of high value to share. So, whitelist my domain RobertRolih.com in your email system, and add me to your contacts to ensure that you get my emails.

*"Engage computers. Prepare for warp speed!"*

– Captain James T. Kirk

# Bonus Chapter

## My Three Best Financial Breakthrough Cheat Codes

The game of life tends to get boring if you are always stuck at the same level.

If you have ever played any platform game on your computer or smartphone, you know that the gameplay consists of advancing from one level, or room, to another harder and more rewarding level, until you win the game.

We can say that life is like a computer game. With one important difference. You only get one shot in real life. Fortunately, in life, there are usually no human eating enemies lurking around when you enter a new room or level. So, your chances of losing your only life are pretty low, and if you are reading this book, it would seem that you survived this far.

A lot of people love computer games and they are very good at them. They like to advance; they like to get new badges; they like a new challenge.

But in real life, most people are stuck at the first or the second level, and they seem to just vegetate there with no real ambition to get anywhere else.

Some people would like to get to the next level, but they can't seem to find the way to do it. They are stuck with no idea on how to move on.

The purpose of this chapter is to give you some great strategies on how to get to the next level in life. If I continue with my computer game analogy, that means that I will give you some cheat codes that you can use right away to advance much faster in life and, eventually, win financially. When you win the financial game of life, everything changes.

You can finally do whatever you want to do, with whom you want and when you want, and that's worth a lot because you only have one life on this Earth. It would be such a waste if you spent it worrying and doing the things that you really didn't like, and don't fulfill you.

A lot has been written about how to achieve personal, business or financial success in life. The advice you can get in any self-help or business book goes like this: dream big, set goals, get rid of the bad habits, think positive, surround yourself with successful people, read books, attend seminars, learn from the best, work hard, eliminate negative emotions, change your beliefs about money, develop a winning mindset, think like an entrepreneur, be determined, focus... and the list goes on and on.

Now, let me tell you something about that advice...

That advice is absolutely on target, and you should absolutely do all these things.

Did you expect me to tell you that all that advice is bull****, and give you an exploding pen that would solve all the problems?

There are no exploding pens in life, but in this chapter, I want to give you three strategies that are not so overused, and widely known as the ones I just mentioned.

Using all the "regular" strategies is great, but let's face it, it doesn't give you a competitive advantage anymore, because there are a lot of people doing all these things already. It's like using shotguns and pistols on the boss at the end of an important level in a computer game. It just doesn't work and you are quickly toast.

To annihilate the boss in a game, you need some special weapons. You need a rail gun, some grenades or a plasma gun. So, let me give you my super special arsenal that I use to win the financial game of life. Get it here: www.MillionDollarDecisionBook.com/bonus

# Acknowledgments

$M$y friend who is in the book publishing business told me that nobody reads this section of the book. So, I guess you are either weird, or you hope to find your name in it. But one thing is sure; my friend was wrong. You are living proof of that.

Writing this book was fun. And even though it was also a lot of hard work, I didn't feel like it was. The main reason is when I was struggling, I started to think about the people whose financial lives would be better because of the ideas in this book. The flow of money from the customers to the financial industry must stop, and a year of hard work is a small price to pay to pursue this cause.

I'd like to thank my wife, Sara Brezigar, without whom I would still be as poor as a church mouse. She is living proof that behind every successful man there is a successful woman. I love you!

Thanks to all my clients who enabled me to build my business and to share the ideas in this book.

Special thanks to my business partners, friends and beta readers, who encouraged me, gave me feedback, ideas or influenced me in the process of writing the book: Paul O'Mahony, Raymond Aaron, Anthony Morrison, Jesse Eker, Anik Singal, Rick Valentine, Fred Lam, Nick James, Matjaž Rekič, Aleksander Šinigoj, Lorand Szasz, Kevin Green, Cheryl Chapman, Daven Michaels, Dan Leman, Paul Preston, Kris Florek, Dave Kettner, Sai Blackbyrn, Carter Thomas, Gavin Ingham, Mody and Nello Acampora, Alexander Apostolov, Simon Coulson, Matthew Kimberley, Vicki Wusche, Jessen James Chinnapan,

Ralph Brogden, Wajed Roger Salam, Jimmy Kim, Ty Cohen, Meta Grošelj, Vaughn Berkeley, Gregor Goslar, Andrej Štesl, Mario Šarčević, Jonathan Herbert, Matthew Moody, Jay Cruiz, Georgy Popovianski, Andreia Hozhan, Mariya Eneva, Robert Kis, Alison Mary, Gregor Grošelj, Andrej Breznik, Matija Rihter, Liviu Paulet, Mat Lock, Andrei Climov, Andrew Majdlik, Matej Fartelj, Mateja Zupan, Pavel Boitor, Andy Manole, Georgy Popovianski, Luka Kogovšek, Nick East, Eamon Mc Grenaghan, Andrej Krt, Darja Bitenc, Daniel Rosca, Dylaan Dowlati, Alen Odzic, Torsten Buder, Harris Vertlieb, David Mihai, Barbara Majcen, William Long, Patrick Harvey, Barbara Hofmeister, Elsie Lim, Gabriel Plesca, Jillian Clarke, Roxanne St. Clair, Andrei Bulimar and many others.

To my publisher, Rob Kosberg and his amazing team, who guided me through the whole process of publishing the book.

To my editor, Kim Thompson-Pinder, from The Raymond Aaron group, who did a great job editing the book and Lisa Kopel, who proofread it.

To my design agency, Vismark, and Dorian Sărmăsan, who came up with the visual design for my brand.

To my designers from the agency Ideasforyou, who created all the cartoons and illustrations in the book. You did an amazing job! And to Dejan Radojičić, who created all the charts and tables.

To my heroes and mentors who influenced my life in a profound way: Brian Tracy, Chet Holmes (rest in peace Chet), Jay Abraham, Frank Kern, Tony Robbins, Warren Buffett, and so on.

To one of the rare good guys in the financial industry, Jack Bogle, who created the low-cost index fund and helped to start the investing revolution.

To Andy Harrington, whose courses helped me to become a better public speaker and to build a successful global business around that.

Super special thank you with a cherry on top to Daniel Priestley, who gave me the idea for the title of the book when we were having lunch. Simply brilliant!

And the last two guys that deserve a special mention... my five-year-old Rupert and three-year-old Rafael, who are my superheroes of inspiration and make me laugh at least ten times a day.

# Notes

1. U.S. Bureau of Economic Analysis (BEA), https://www.bea.gov/

2. "5,300 Wells Fargo employees fired over 2 million phony accounts", Money.Cnn.com, September 9, 2016. http://money.cnn.com/2016/09/08/investing/wells-fargo-created-phony-accounts-bank-fees/

3. "5 Years Ago Bernie Madoff Was Sentenced to 150 Years In Prison – Here's How His Scheme Worked", BusinessInsider.com, July 1, 2014, http://www.businessinsider.com/how-bernie-madoffs-ponzi-scheme-worked-2014-7

4. "Paulson Event-Driven Fund Said to End Last Year Down 36%", Bloomberg.com, January 11, 2015. https://www.bloomberg.com/news/articles/2015-01-11/paulson-event-driven-fund-said-to-end-last-year-down-36-

5. You can get the complete methodology and results of the study at http://www.cxoadvisory.com/gurus/

6. "Average annual hours actually worked per worker", Stats.Oecd.org, https://stats.oecd.org/Index.aspx?DataSetCode=ANHRS

7. "Tyson's Bankruptcy Is a Lesson In Ways to Squander a Fortune", NYtimes.com, August 5, 2003. http://www.nytimes.com/2003/08/05/sports/tyson-s-bankruptcy-is-a-lesson-in-ways-to-squander-a-fortune.html

8. "Mike Tyson Opens Up on 'The View'", ABC news, May 7 2010. http://abcnews.go.com/Entertainment/mike-tyson-opens-view/story?id=10566489

9. "Entrepreneurship and the U.S. Economy", BLS.gov, https://www.bls.gov/bdm/entrepreneurship/entrepreneurship.htm

10. Nassim Nicholas Taleb, The Black Swan: The Impact of the Highly Improbable (Random House, 2010).

11. To learn more about Maslow's Hierarchy of Needs visit http://www.simplypsychology.org/maslow.html

12. Social Security Fact Sheet, June 2016, SSA.gov,
    https://www.ssa.gov/news/press/factsheets/basicfact-alt.pdf

13. US bankruptcy court statistics, UScourts.gov

14. "Medical bills underlie 60 percent of U.S. bankrupts: study", Reuters.com,
    June 4, 2009. http://www.reuters.com/article/us-healthcare-bankruptcy-
    idUSTRE5530Y020090604

15. Annual United States Road Crash Statistics, 2016, ASIRT.org,
    http://asirt.org/initiatives/informing-road-users/road-safety-facts/road-crash-statistics

16. Ben Goldacre, Bad Science (HarperCollins, 2008).

17. "How much gold has been mined?", World Gold Council, Gold.com.
    http://www.gold.org/gold-mining/what-gold-mining-companies-produce/
    how-much-gold-has-been-mined

18. "Germany's hyperinflation-phobia", Economist.com, November 15, 2013.
    http://www.economist.com/blogs/freeexchange/2013/11/economic-history-1

19. Comparison Of Prices Over 70 Years, 2013, ThePeopleHistory.com

20. Fortune 500 Archive, Archive.Fortune.com

21. "Can Stock Market Forecasters Forecast?", Alfred Cowles 3rd, December 31, 1932.

22. Laurent Barras, Olivier Scaillet and Russell Wermers, False Discoveries in Mutual
    Fund Performance: Measuring Luck in Estimated Alphas, February 2010 (The
    Journal of Finance)

23. Brad M. Barber and Terrance Odean, The Behavior of Individual Investors, 2013,
    Handbook of the Economics of Finance

24. "Ownership of Mutual Funds, Shareholder Sentiment, and Use of the Internet",
    October 2016, Investment Company Institute Research Perspective

25. Allan S. Roth, How a Second Grader Beats Wall Street: Golden Rules Any Investor
    Can Learn (Wiley, 2011).

26. "Leverage as High as 50-1 Lures OTC Forex Traders Who Mostly Lose",
    November 12, 2014, Bloomberg.com. https://www.bloomberg.com/news/
    articles/2014-11-12/leverage-as-high-as-50-1-lures-otc-forex-traders-who-mostly-lose

27. Commodity Futures Trading Commission, CTFC.gov

28. "Foreign currency trading is easy — an easy way to lose money", LAtimes.com, April 03, 2011. http://articles.latimes.com/2011/apr/03/business/la-fi-amateur-currency-trading-20110403

29. Barber, Lee, Liu and Odean, The Behavior of Individual Investors, 2011

30. "Entrepreneurship and the U.S. Economy", BLS.gov, https://www.bls.gov/bdm/entrepreneurship/entrepreneurship.htm

31. U.S. Census Bureau, www.census.gov

32. Robert Greene, Mastery (Penguin Books, 2013).

33. "Warren Buffett's Frugal, So Why Aren't You?", Investopedia.com, 2016. http://www.investopedia.com/articles/financialcareers/10/buffett-frugal.asp

# About Robert Rolih

Robert's mission is to share what the financial industry doesn't want us to know about investing. With his simple investing system, you will be able to outperform the pros while spending only a couple of hours per YEAR on investing.

Robert grew up in a poor backwater village in a small country, became a successful entrepreneur, (cooperating with people like Chet Holmes and Brian Tracy) and then lost most of his money because he trusted financial advisers and financial "gurus." That inspired him to invest seven years of his life to research what is going on behind the scenes of the financial industry.

Today Robert's goal is to give you the right investing education and help you avoid the costly mistakes that most investors make. His live and online training programs have saved millions of dollars for more than 40,000 clients all around the world.

Robert lives in a scenic hillside village in the middle of a forest with his wife, Sara, and his two children, Rupert and Rafael.

## Connect with Robert

Make sure that you subscribe to Robert's newsletter, where he shares his wisdom about investing and money making. Do that at www.RobertRolih.com.

You can also join his 50,000+ followers on Facebook at https://www.facebook.com/robertrolihpublicspeaker/

For more information about Robert's **online and live training programs** and how to book him as a **speaker** visit www.RobertRolih.com.

ROBERT ROLIH
*Fast forward your wealth*